HUMANISTIC PSYCHOLOGY:
Interviews with
Maslow, Murphy,
and Rogers

STUDIES OF THE PERSON

edited by

Carl R. Rogers
William R. Coulson

HUMANISTIC PSYCHOLOGY:
Interviews with Maslow, Murphy, and Rogers

Willard B. Frick

Albion College

CHARLES E. MERRILL PUBLISHING COMPANY
A Bell & Howell Company   Columbus, Ohio

International Standard Book Number: 0–675–09966–8

Library of Congress Catalog Card Number: 79–160221

1 2 3 4 5 6 7 8 9 10 – 75 74 73 72 71

In memory of Abraham Maslow.   1908–1970

FOREWORD

Let me tell you the value of Willard Frick's interviews for me: they caught my attention, as often a person will while a presentation will not. The person will always be more interesting than his theory. Getting people to say how things are for them is what I am going to claim psychology ought to be about for now anyway.

If it's true for you, too, that persons are more interesting than theories, if they engage your attention spontaneously while abstract theory engages you only if you're already engaged, then this book can be valuable to you. Through dealing with the persons of three great psychologists, it can *introduce* you to some issues presently important in what is called humanistic psychology and ought better to be simply human psychology.

The example of the men Dr. Frick explores, men who are using the language of the time and the subject to go beyond words and into ideas, may cause you to be more of a person yourself, thinking your own thoughts, making your own theories and testing them. We have too much now of people going around saying "peak experience" or "congruence," rendering their lives or explaining the lives of their neighbors in the words of Abraham Maslow or Carl Rogers, adopting new and coercive alienisms, worse than the older school psychologies for their inherent easy appeal and thus their imprecision. If the traditional psychology, to which in part the new humanism stands as a rebellion, was excessively technical, at least in so being it discouraged the development of a large cadre of camp followers, all of whom speak to one another no more sensibly than before, only in a new, self-righteous, inbred code: "I've peaked Have you peaked?"

As opposed to the older, cautious psychology (which I can call "school psychology" because school is where you're taught to do your work carefully even if at the price of working in irrelevancies) the problems dealt with by humanistic innovators, the men in this book, are substantial and human-concerned; they are the problems which people live. And as opposed to the sloppy sloganeering of the camp followers, the work of the innovators has methodological interest too: for these men want to be no less rigorous in their work for dealing with interesting, human problems; they want always to work things out (you'll see this so clearly in the interviews), not just to repeat what they've heard.

The task of working things out in a human psychology is imposing. For now each innovator seems to have his own vocabulary of problem responses, and one job younger workers in the field will want to take on—Willard Frick tackles it in this book—is to find the common notes in each set of responses, for eventually we will need a common vocabulary in order to mount an effective research campaign on human problems.

The greatest need of the new human psychology, you see, is for an effective method of checking knowledge claims. If we have no standards for specifying satisfactory approximations of truth in a human psychology then we will have no way of moving past our first set of problems and likely will content ourselves with asserting that at least we care about the right problems—eventually an enterprise only of foolish, lazy men. Without a common method there can be no research corps, other than one which locks itself in yet another school. And then psychology again will have laid aside its public responsibility.

As an alternative to prolonging the period of claiming that we care, let me suggest that we begin to gather systematic evidence in human psychology and that we begin our quest for evidence at very elementary places: that we ask people, for example, what they care about. Perhaps my own assertion early in this foreword can be of this nature: i.e., count one individual (me) who is more interested in people than in summaries of theory. And then let's start counting noses—except they won't be counted simply, for people often don't ell the truth at first; you have to stay with them long enough to find out what they really mean.

How do you get information about what human beings are like? *First you ask them.* Ask me what I'm like and I'll tell you as best I know—if I don't think you're using me and if I can get around to trusting you and if I think you've good reason to know and if you hang in with me long enough (for the best things I might be able to say can't be said quickly or easily; at first I don't even know I have them in me to say).

This then—to ask, to hang in there, and even to reveal something of himself—is the beginning Willard Frick has made in his interviews. What is Abraham Maslow like, and Gardner Murphy, and Carl Rogers?

Read on.

William R. Coulson

La Jolla, California
June, 1971

PREFACE

I would like to make some brief comments concerning the organization of this book. The interviews are considered to be the major focus and are, therefore, presented first. The interviews are then followed by three supplementary chapters designed to enrich and amplify the interview material by presenting, as a theoretical context, a humanistic-holistic orientation to personality. The reader is invited to read the interviews first and then, if sufficiently stimulated, proceed to the theoretical chapters which follow. This format and suggestion is arbitrary, however, and some may prefer to approach the book by reading the theoretical chapters first, as background, and then move on to the more personal material of the interviews. From another point of view, of course, the important thing for an author is to have his book read—from any direction.

I must confess that I am indebted to many people and in a variety of ways. This book represents a revision of portions of an unpublished dissertation. I feel most fortunate to have had Roger Howell, Warren A. Ketcham, Howard Y. McClusky, and G. Max Wingo to serve on my doctoral committee and to have received their support for a study that did not tread the well-worn path of most doctoral research. Their interest and support throughout the study was an important source of strength to me. The sensitivity, kindness, and respect that I received from my Chairman, Professor Warren A. Ketcham, leaves me with a deep sense of gratitude and affection. He gave wise council and valuable suggestions, but never wavered in his trust in my ability, my judgment, and my integrity. The spirit that emerged from this relationship and within this learning climate proved invaluable to my efforts at creative scholarship and my desire to have aspects of my individuality maintain a forceful presence throughout the work.

I would like to take this opportunity also, to express my appreciation for the financial support I received. This study, in its entirety, was supported by Grant No. OEG–59–325076–0004 from the Office of Education, U.S. Department of Health, Education, and Welfare, under the title "An Analysis of Total Personality as Advocated by Holistic Theorists and its Effect upon Healthy Personality." As stipulated by the grant, my research also received cost-sharing support from Albion College. It was the generous assistance of this grant that enabled me not only to pursue the study itself, but allowed me to undertake the personal interviews with Dr. Abraham Maslow, Dr. Gardner Murphy, and Dr. Carl Rogers that form the major portion of this book. As indicated later, these men were most hospitable and gracious in their response to my request for personal interviews and they gave themselves fully to my project. Their time and generosity are deeply appreciated.

A special expression of appreciation goes to Mrs. Sally Barcus of Charles E. Merrill for her personal enthusiasm for this book and for her special skills that guided it into being. A word of thanks is extended to Mrs. Mary Jane Abbott who did much of the "busy" work and typing in the final stages of the manuscript.

Willard B. Frick

Albion College
June, 1971

CONTENTS

part **1**

Tragedy and human suffering abound and stalk the earth like an ancient plague. The trial is over and the verdict is clear. Social systems and their institutional supports are out of touch with human experience, human longings, and human needs. Yes, out of touch with human nature. The prevailing personality of our time, the "normal" in our culture, is virtually schizophrenic. He is fragmented between futile efforts to maintain the principal source of personal significance via his past meanings and allegiance to dehumanizing, anachronistic value systems and his struggles in sad and perverse ways to maintain the integrity of the human spirit. And we must remember that we share this personality. We have, most of us, become caricatures of humanness and our lives are rarely lived in fullness and in harmony with our potentials. Man's own inner and personal discord burdens him with a tragic inability to relate to others in a spirit of love and mutuality. Interpersonal bonds are more likely to be forged in hate, in obligation, in guilt, in selfishness and exploitation. Relationships attenuate, closing off their possibilities before they have scarcely begun. Alienation and disaffection, personal and interpersonal, is a fact, a way of life. We live among strangers and enemies, even when we are alone.

At all levels of society, in all its institutions, and in most human dimensions of experience, we are in a transition of crisis propor-

3

tions. The ethics, morality and belief systems upon which old orders and erstwhile conceptual organizations have received their support are no longer viable. Yet, in an anachronistic sense they are heavy handed upon us, upon the present; stifling and diverting the flow of creative life forces that form the very basis of selfhood, personal identity, and sanity. Slowly and subtly we have become insensitive and, en masse, must share the guilt as integral components of our dehumanizing[1] social machinery and the complicated institutional structure which supports such a closed system.

THE INTIMIDATION OF EXPERIENCE

Basically and on more intimate terms the crisis we are in can be viewed or conceptualized as a crisis of personal experience. We are in a revolutionary era that does not easily permit one to sense with any degree of certainty the validity of his observations and "outer" experience or feel the integrity and reality of inner or personal experience. Yet, this confusion over the reality and meaning of experience has not led to the emergence of new meanings and to integrations derived from the interaction of shared experience, but has hardened into what I shall refer to as the intimidation of experience; the need to compete for its validity and significance.

The intimidation of experience goes on at all levels of human intercourse; between parent and child, husband and wife, teacher and pupil, and patient and therapist. Perhaps these role-centered relationships as I have stated them, i.e., parent-child, husband-wife, reflect this problem.

---

[1] The use of the word dehumanizing has gradually become a meaningless, cheap coin of reference that mocks our common experience of profound suffering, frustration, despair, alienation, and human denial. It is frequently used without real sensitivity or awareness of the social *process* that is such an integral feature of the dehumanization of men in our society. We are unaware, too, of the complex web of institutional support this process receives within our social systems. Without awareness, we have become so very much a part of its evil. Also, the use of the term "dehumanize" seldom explicates its most important implication. In the *American College Dictionary* "dehumanize" is defined as follows: To "deprive of human character." There is the implication, here, that there are certain intrinsic human qualities, characteristics, needs, etc., that define "humanness," a central core of ennobling attributes or potentials of the human personality that persist and emerge as cardinal features of the *humanization* process.

Rather than a sharing and an interaction of my experience with your experience so that we may understand and develop a mutual respect for our unique experiential selves and bring into being an enlarged and enriched sense of awareness and reality, it is more often that we struggle in competition for the validity of our experience. It becomes my experience vs. your experience, like two teams engaged in a contest for the highest score. And if your experience is too deviant, therefore too threatening to my experience, your experience then must be suspect and "treated"; evaluated, ridiculed, rejected, diagnosed, analyzed, or even drugged. As the intimidation of experience operates in government circles, William Fulbright once called it the "mummyfication of opinion."

Children, the lesser powers, are often told what to experience, what was experienced, what they should experience. Most parent-child relationships are based upon this formula of intimidation until children become so estranged from their own inner processes and from the intuitive sensitivity to the validity of their own experience that they either go "crazy" in hate and self-denial or rebel in defiance against such flagrant violations to these most intimate aspects of selfhood.

It is not so incredible however that the youth should emerge in the vanguard of the creation of a new moral consciousness for our time, and bring an articulation of new forms and expressions of awareness for our society. New and higher forms of social reality are beginning to emerge. Most adults, nevertheless, remain linked to the past with incredible rigidity, impervious to these changing realities and unable for the most part to alter themselves; unable to receive the social and moral messages, and respond to these insights with some emotional openness and commitment that would lead to personal change and ultimately to social change as well.

We need to develop a new concept of parent-child interaction; that of *reciprocal socialization*. This concept would encourage the notion that parents should be open to change and, in fact, socialized by their children instead of perceiving their role solely in terms of the responsibility for the socialization of their children. How many parents are significantly influenced by their children?

Perhaps the most institutionalized, rigidly entrenched and destructive form of the intimidation of experience is to be found in education, where from kindergarten through the graduate schools, this control, manipulation, and intimidation of experience is built into the very essense and structure of the system. In fact, the smooth and proper functioning of the educational establishment depends upon it and, therefore, encourages it. Most examinations, the system of grades, and traditional methods of teaching all serve as instruments of experience control and intimidation. Effective education must involve a process and function as an interpersonal enterprise of shared, multi-dimensional flow of experience.

New perspectives on role relationships and interpersonal experience must evolve that will redefine these rigid, structured relationships that depend upon the domination and imposition of one person's perceptions and experience upon another's. Parent-child, child-adult, husband-wife, male-female, teacher-pupil, doctor-patient, patient-therapist, black-white, and perhaps others, are all in need of liberation from the rigid role definitions that encourage and support the intimidation of experience.

The denial of experience is perhaps the most basic level of human rejection for it is a denial of the human composition and the most intimate aspects of the evolving self-structure. To confirm another person, to support and authenticate his worth, is achieved at a deep level of shared interaction and experience, and leads to an expanding awareness of self and others.

✧   ✧   ✧   ✧   ✧

The discipline of psychology has been strangely silent and reluctant to address itself to these real and complex human problems; to the existential dilemmas in human experience and interpersonal relationships. Pursuing an outdated concept of science, psychologists have chosen a less courageous, and less creative path of operationalism where only neatly measurable, quantifiable behavior is considered respectable subject matter and worthy of the weight of this science and its sophisticated methodology. By and large, modern psychology has become scholarly, yet pedantic; sophisticated, yet irrelevant; highly professional, yet largely ignorant and insensitive to the subject of its endeavor, the human person. Historically, psychologists have fought a long and hard battle for respectability and it is partially this struggle for recognition and professional status that has led to such an ironic situation. Psychologists are notoriously "science conscious" and defensive about their status as "scientists." Few psychologists, plagued with such personal insecurity and the status problems of their profession, are without highly visible and reassuring copies of the respected technical journal *Science*[2] on their desks. Thus, the defensive and self-conscious concern regarding status has led more and more psychologists into highly circumscribed areas of concern and to a pursuit of research problems that are very respectable, quite well-managed methodologically, relatively easily controlled to yield solid, quantifiable results, yet notably out of the context of man's experience and the important internal data that issue forth from his experience. Thus, the vital concerns and experiences of most men that weave the fabric and design of their personalities and determine the course of their lives are largely ignored in psychological research and by psychologists, except for a courageous few. As we move closer and closer to man's inner experience and the creative and idiosyncratic methods and interpretations necessary to understand this experience, we enter a whole new, unexplored world of myths and meanings, personal values, creative symbolism and imagery, unique perceptions, and inevitably, we move into the spiritual realm.

The issues and problems growing out of this inner world of experience as they are translated and reified by the individual represent the breadth and depth of the human personality and the most crucial issues in life. Life's polarities emerge; love and hate, life and death, joy and sorrow, stability and change, creativity and conformity, responsibility and dependency, all assume tensional relationships that must be opened to awareness. These life concerns are but a few of the areas that our traditional behavioristically oriented psychology has chosen to ignore in favor of more easily defined and managed problems. Psychology and the traditional experimental approaches to personality theory appear inappropriately academic and remote from this great personal and social upheaval we are experiencing and the human problems and suffering that result.

---

[2] Official publication of the American Association for the Advancement of Science.

Some major concepts of man, current in psychological theory, have yet to fully humanize man or take into account his complete nature and the full range of his potentials and inner resources. These limited views and theories prefer to see man as the determined and hapless victim of a complex reinforcement history, as the pawn in a contest between unconscious psychic forces and external social pressures or, at best, respected as a complicated machine and perhaps perceived as a computer model with such terms as "input," "storage," "output" and "retrieval" applied to complicated neural and psychological processes and systems.

With a keener and more balanced perspective we are beginning to realize that Freud's genius left a legacy of mixed blessing, providing us with new and dramatic insights into human motivation and behavior while at the same time, laying the theoretical and philosophical foundation for a pessimistic view of man's nature and its possibilities. It has encouraged many, many people to adopt a personal philosophy of pessimism and irresponsibility.

Man, under the Freudian mystique, virtually loses control of his own life directions, and at best, may only determine the sublimations that serve as the ultimate resolutions in the inexorable duel between social forces and the instinctual impulses. In this view, man is destined to wage a dreary, life long, rearguard action against conflict. Pleasure seeking and tension reduction are sovereign motivations.

Psychiatrists, as well as many, many non-medical therapists, i.e., social workers, have inherited this legacy and are a good example of a professional group caught in the current storm of clashing visions, philosophies, and conflicting views of man. Psychiatrists, with rare exception, are in a serious personal and professional crisis in their relationship to the existential agony and the spiritual vacuum expressed as "meaninglessness" which plague the majority of patients who, in a not-so-quiet desperation, reach out for something of substance to relate to, something with form and meaning, perhaps even for the touch of a warm and loving human response. In subtle and symbolic ways, these needs emerge as major themes that are communicated on another level by the more overt expressions of frustration, personal tragedy, a sense of life unfulfilled.

Psychiatrists, like most of us confronting the cataclysmic forces of change today, are trapped between a past of crumbling icons, falling heroes, and a world of new demands and changing reality. Many, sensing their confusion and the inappropriateness of their theory and techniques to meet the needs of the strangers in their offices, renew their faith in an outdated medical model of man's predicament, prescribing and relying more and more frequently on symptom control via drug therapy. When theoretical issues cannot be avoided, they fall back in a regression of spirit and courage to those Freudian concepts that alleviate their anxiety and provide a supportive theoretical structure for their work. Others, more disillusioned with the efficacy of psychoanalysis, drift into a nondirective somnolence that represents an outdated and inappropriate application of Rogerian techniques of twenty years ago.

Behaviorism, too, the very foundation of modern psychology, has pursued and helped create a limited vision of man. This school of psychology conceives of man as a complex machine with its closed system of part-functions and static regularity. Man is built upon a hierarchy of stimulus-response organization leading to predictable habit patterns, and *reinforcement* is the key word to personality development. Indeed, the behavioristic model and its applications have become so familiar that the term *reinforcement* seems to be competing with the Freudian lexicon of such terms as repression, the unconscious, oedipus complex, etc. Implicitly, there is the assumption, for all operational purposes, that man does not have a veridical nature distinct and autonomous from the social, shaping, and programming influences impinging upon him.

Are we to deny or ignore the possibility that such pervasive philosophies and models of the human personality have no determining influence within a society on man's perceptions of himself, and his possibilities? Such a suggestion is irresponsible naiveté. There can be little doubt that man's experience and definition of himself, his interpretation of the nature of reality, particularly inner reality, and its personal and interpersonal implications is going to be influenced, in part, by the broad, sweeping, and pervasive Zietgiest which prevails in a given era and society regarding man, his nature, and his potentials.

HUMANISTIC PSYCHOLOGY

I have often been asked by interested colleagues and friends to explain the nature and meaning of humanistic psychology. This is no easy task, for the answer is not a simple one and the question cannot be answered in a doctrinaire fashion by resorting to the glib statement of some formula or methodology. Humanistic psychology, a vigorous "third force" in psychology, has emerged as a passionate expression of protest against the limited and limiting images of man expounded by the two other major schools of psychology, psychoanalysis and behaviorism. While not denying their important contributions, humanistic psychology holds to the position that the images of man presented by these two theoretical systems are, like pages torn from a book, only parts that contribute to a greater whole and are therefore incomplete. Humanistic psychology, however, also presents us with a more positive philosophical position and, in the final analysis, represents a psychology with certain characteristic commitments of its own as to the nature of man and the nature and scope of that science which is necessary to explore and acquire a broader, more profound understanding of man. This philosophical position of humanistic psychology places man, the human person and his experience, at the center of its concern. Its priorities are then determined by the authentic human problems which emerge, sharply focused, into view. Humanistic psychology is extremely sensitive and resistant to the seductive temptation to model man after a theory rather than fashion a theory that more fully reveals man and is in closer harmony with man and his nature. The former instance is often like putting clothes into a suitcase that is too small. The clothes must be pushed, arranged, and rearranged and perhaps, before we are through, we must even eliminate an important item or two so we can close our bag successfully. This analogy seems appropriate to represent our traditional images of man and the distortions that become intrinsic characteristics in order to preserve crucial and sacrosanct elements in a theoretical system.

With man at the center, however, and with no need to deny or distort his many characteristics and possibilities for the purpose of preserving a theoretical structure, humanistic psychology has retained a greater measure of freedom to concentrate on significant human problems and concerns that can take man's full range of inner experience into serious account.

part ||

The three personal interviews presented in this book, as well as the theoretical chapters in Part 3, represent selected and revised material from the author's unpublished dissertation, "A Holistic Theory of Healthy Personality," University of Michigan, 1969. Originally, seven personality theorists were identified as holistic in their philosophical posture and in their orientation to the study of the person. The theorists selected were Gordon Allport, Andreas Angyal, Kurt Goldstein, Prescott Lecky, Abraham Maslow, Gardner Murphy, and Carl Rogers. The primary purpose of the study was to analyze the substantive writings of these seven theorists and move to a final synthesis and presentation of a holistic theory of healthy personality. As an enrichment to this dissertation research, personal interviews were planned to be held with the four living theorists represented in my study: Allport, Maslow, Murphy, and Rogers. The unfortunate death of Gordon Allport left me with the three interviews contained herein.

My purpose, therefore, in carrying out the interviews was to enrich my formal research with as much substantive material as I could obtain directly from the living theorists in my study. At the same time, I wanted to establish real contact with the personalities of the men responsible for the theories. Theories, per se, are likely to represent highly abstract expressions of the personalities who de-

veloped or created them. This is particularly true, I believe, of personality theories. For this reason I did my best to avoid a highly formal and structured interview schedule that would promote increased objectivity and encourage higher levels of abstraction at
the expense of establishing a genuine acquaintance and interaction
with the personality of the theorist. I wanted the interviews to take
their own unique course and individual form so that each person
could emerge within our encounter as a sensitive, living, breathing
human being. I wanted the personality as well as the theory to
come alive during the interview.

There were times, of course, when these two purposes were in
conflict and I was faced with a choice between a formal pursuit of a
technical or theoretical issue or a yielding to more spontaneous and
intimate personal expressions and reflections. It is the balance between these that I feel was achieved that makes these interviews
significantly different and worthy of availability to a wider au-
dience.

In each interview there emerged, each in its own way, a genuine dialogue and on occasion our interaction together reached
peak moments of spontaniety, intimacy, and private sharing that is
rare to achieve in such formal interviews: The sadness we both felt
when Dr. Maslow discussed the many restrictions he had imposed
upon his life in order to devote himself more completely to his writings and theory building; Dr. Rogers' expression of pride and pleasure over his very close relationship with his oldest granddaughter;
and Dr. Murphy's emphasis on his early, intense, and continuing
dedication to psychical research as well as his brief spark of irrita-
tion and rejection of the suggestion when asked if he had ever enjoyed a "peak" experience as Maslow describes the phenomenon.
But on other levels, the interviews which follow contain many
things of interest and value in addition to these personal insights
and vignettes. There are discussions drawing upon the valuable experience and knowledgeable perspective of these three men on a
wide range of pertinent topics including education, psychotherapy,
drug usage among young people, concepts of the healthy personality, recent gains in psychical research, human growth and constructive change, the value of T-groups, the student disorder and chaos

on college campuses, and judgments on the current status of psychology with predictions regarding the future developments of the discipline. Finally, in addition, the reader will encounter the more theory-centered questions and responses that involve a discussion of contemporary issues and details that are difficult to pursue outside of a personal interview. At each level of engagement and participation it is hoped that these interviews with three of the most esteemed psychologists of our time will be a valuable addition to the growing literature of humanistic psychology and, in addition, will prove to be a source of pleasure and stimulation to students of psychology and especially those interested in the broad area of personality theory.

It was an unbelieveably arduous and time consuming task to move from the taped interviews to the final edited manuscript. Readability, of course, had to be considered, but it was the necessity of maintaining as accurate and authentic a presentation of the interview experience as possible that received priority. At times, therefore, readability was sacrificed to maintain the intimate, conversational character of the interview which was the primary quality we wished to preserve.

One final word. It was a rare privilege, indeed one of my finest experiences, to sit down with these three men in an atmosphere of sharing, mutual trust, and respect. Three characteristics stand out in my mind as I think of these men in a collective sense; they were gentle, humble, and sensitive, and I was unable to discern a trace of condescension during our conversations. It is neither a profound nor original observation, but it seems to me that these qualities are among the distinguishing features of great men.

1

Interview with
Dr. Abraham Maslow

Frick: Dr. Maslow, the beginning of your career goes back into the early 30s, and as I looked at some of your early published works, it seemed to me that you were at one time a very traditional psychologist although I don't think you were as behavioristic as many were at that time, but at any rate, you were a respected member of the establishment. Now you are leading a third force psychology that has really been extremely free-wheeling and experimental in its efforts to grow beyond the deficiencies of traditional psychology, and I'm wondering where along the way in your career you sensed these deficiencies in psychology and where along the way you developed the more humanistic concerns that you are expressing now.

Maslow: Well, I think the humanistic concerns were part of the reason, a very large part of the reason that I went into psychology at all, from philosophy. My concerns were socialistic with American Socialism. Norman Thomas was a great hero of mine, and Upton Sinclair, and Eugene Debs, in college. There is the Jewish tradition of the utopian, and the ethical and I was pretty definitely looking for the improvement of mankind. I became impatient with philosophy, at all the talking that didn't get anyplace, and wanted in effect an empirical philosophy in the old 19th century sense of working at philosophical problems empirically. I had made one shot at it before at Cornell with Titchener, and then just fled.

Frick: Did you hope to find what you were looking for in the psychology of the day?

Maslow: Well, I had, when I came into it, because I knew nothing of psychology. I came in following a kind of an ideal which didn't yet exist. But, I was fascinated with everything that *did* exist and also behaviorism just looked different then than it does now. Clearly the great moment when I went back into psychology was when I read Watson's work and had a great illumination, a great

19

vision about the future. You know, this was a programatic thing and it looked so clear.

Frick: Behaviorism really appealed to you at the time?

Maslow: Oh, yes, That brought me into psychology, or back into it, because it looked as if all you needed was hard work and so on. The future looked quite clear. There was a program that all you do is condition everything, etc. But, as a student, I ran across Freud and Adler out there at Wisconsin. The first paper I did was on psychoanalysis, but I was a very timid boy—very shy, very easily frightened, very isolated—an outsider, and the first paper I did was for the Wisconsin Academy of Arts and Sciences. I think I was a first-year graduate student, and I offered a paper which would still be worthy of doing. It was called "Psychoanalysis and Mental Hygiene as Status Quo Social Philosophy." And I was to give that, but when the day came I was so frightened, so timid, that I just fled. I just didn't show up for the meeting and didn't give my paper, but that was the first paper I . . . you know, if I *had* given it, that would have been the first paper I would have published. So that I felt open about psychology from the very beginning and used it in terms of an ideal which did not yet exist. Some people are frightened away by the inadequacies of psychology, that is, the discrepancy between what exists and the ideal.

Frick: Many students are today . . .

Maslow: Right, but I think the best students are not. I think I was a good student, but I felt that if psychology did not come up to the ideal, well damn it, it should. And so I went into it having what we now call humanistic questions very definitely in mind. As a matter of fact, behaviorism looked like a program for humanism then, and it was only when it played itself out—when it didn't work out—that I became disenchanted. But I was never, you know, the devotee, the disciple, the great programmatic follower . . . my dissertation really came out of my studies of Adler and Freud and it was an effort to answer the question which was right?

I should say at the other end, too, that I feel quite open about . . . I'm not anti-behavioristic except as a philosophy. And I don't feel sectarian about it at all. The humanistic psychology that I'm working up, and I hope to make systematic, includes, that is, it s a larger philosophical, theoretical, and methodological structure which includes the whole positivistic psychology. It doesn't reject t.

rick: It incorporates it and makes a better use of it perhaps, theoretically?

Maslow: That's right.

rick: I hope to get to that theoretical integration in a few minutes. You know, Dr. Maslow, something that interests me ties in with the question I was going to ask you. You said you were a very timid boy, very obsequious, perhaps, in your early graduate work. Does this have any bearing on your later and more recent concerns or self-actualization? Certainly, as much as anyone I know, your theories are very much a part of you as a person and so I wonder if this represents personal striving.

Maslow: That can be answered at many levels. In going through psychoanalysis you discover all sorts of things. I guess at the most superficial level, the most conscious level and obvious level, this self-actualization idea came from simply loving and admiring two people in particular, and then later more. One was Ruth Benedict and one was Max Wertheimer, teachers whom I just loved in a way that today's students don't love their teachers. But they were puzzling. They didn't fit. It was as if they came from another planet or something. Everything I knew didn't explain them. They were mysteries. They were also very nice and parental with me, and answered questions and let me hang around. It was just simply the normal kind of—normal for me, anyway—sort of intellectual poking, poking, poking, until I understood. And I had all sorts of notes on them, sort of journal notes, and I kept on trying to figure them out. That was an entirely personal enterprise. It didn't even occur to me to think of it as an exploration or a research. It would be like sort of a diary occupation, and I lectured to my classes about these ideas since my classes were always the repository for whatever I happened to be interested in at the time. And then one day, finally, those two pictures clicked into one, and there was a composite rather than just individuals. Of course I was very excited about that and I kept on plugging away privately, secretly. It didn't fit into the Zeitgeist at all, and the only use I made of it was lecturing to my

classes and discussions with my friends. Then the only reason it be
came public was through Werner Wolff who was a very brilliar
depth psychologist at the time. He had just started a journal an
asked me for this material and it was published about seven yea;
after it was written.

Frick: Well, he published one of your first writings on your exper
ments with the self-actualizing or healthy personality, didn't he?

Maslow: That was *the* first publication and I think I would hav
been too timid to do it unless he had urged me and asked me for i
because it was so "unscientific." But his journal was called—yo
know—it wasn't like Psychological Review or the Journal of Exper
mental Psychology. It was called "Personality Studies," or som
thing like that, and this gave me the courage to do it, to write it, t
publish it, to make it available.

Frick: That hasn't been many years ago, really, has it?

Maslow: No, that was published, oh, it must have been about 194
or somewhere around there, but it had been sitting on my des
since 1936 or 1937.

Frick: Still timid?

Maslow: Oh, yes. Well, a little of it still pops up once in awhile.

Frick: . . . I can't believe that now!

Maslow: Well, in my dreams and fantasies the little boy is sti
there.

❀   ❀   ❀   ❀   ❀

Frick: Dr. Maslow, I've been a follower of yours for many yea;
now, and I think that your writings have had a great deal to do wit
my own efforts and my own position, and so it's difficult for me t
really offer a critical and objective appraisal, I think, as many cou]
who are less involved with your writings and thinking, but I wou]
like to play the devil's advocate with some of my questions for
few minutes. I think as I've gotten deeper into your work in the la:
few months, I have been disturbed a bit by the very strong emphɑ
sis you give to an instinctoid base for man's behavior and deve
opment. It's as though you are introducing a biological determir
ism here and I think this is seen when you use the analogy: Mɑ
actualizes his potentials in a very similar way to the acorn becon

ing an oak. You use this analogy, or similar ones, very frequently. Somehow I see here, and I think the thing that really bothers me, is that I see a real programming here. Certainly, the model of the acorn into the oak suggests an indelible kind of programming and this troubles me, and I would like you to respond to it, and then I have some related issues that I would like to get into. Maybe it troubles you, too. I don't know.

Maslow: Trouble isn't exactly the word—fascinated with perhaps. Yes, I love thinking about them—working at it—I try to work it out. I think the acorn-oak business was a poor choice of figures of speech, of analogies, because it *is* programmed.

Frick: It did lead to that connotation?

Maslow: That's right. It just leads to the notion of something growing all by itself without any effort, and it's quite clear that you have to put something together with what I'm convinced are instinct-like or genetic or biologically based potentialities, very, very weak, very delicate, very subtle, not like animal or plant things. We have an inner sense of strength, and of overwhelmingness and practically nothing can stop a cat from becoming a cat but melding into this nature is the existential emphasis on man making himself. That is, I would think of the potentialities of human nature as being biologically rooted or instinctoid, but that it's in the culture and in one's own life and with will and self-responsibility that one makes oneself. That is—the potentialities—if you leave them alone you are just a vegetable, so that hard work is the path to becoming a good physician or scientist, or whatever; hard work, determination, commitment and incorporating the ego ideal into the self. I think the easiest way to say it is in the existentialist mode of saying "man is his own project," only they overdo it, because they become anti-biological.

Frick: That's right, they do, but I feel there is a real contradiction here, in a sense, in your position. I haven't worked it out yet but I've been struggling with it. You say that we've got to discover this nature. It's there but we've got to discover it. The existentialists come along and say "No, we really haven't got to discover it, we've got to create it." Now, it seems to me that in your position, you are somehow de-emphasizing choice.

Maslow: I don't mean to.

Frick: You don't mean to?

Maslow: No. That was why I said that was a poor choice of words. There is no word that puts together discover-create. It's sort of a difficult discovering or if I think of, let's say my working as a psychotherapist, of the difficulty with which one discovers one's human nature, or one's own talents, or tendencies or tastes, or trends or constitutional-temperamental bent—then we must make up some suitable words, because that's the operation. That's the basic operation upon which I'd start this whole business of uncovering, discovering, creating by hard work and by one's own determination of oneself with, however, the receptive emphasis. That is, the creating is *not* arbitrary. I cannot make myself into a woman, except in a very inefficient and unsatisfactory way. The real job there, is in a certain sense, discovering what you are and that phrase is okay with all these other modifications, you know, discovering your own trends, your own bent, your own tendencies, your own intentions and then sort of bringing them to pass. If I discover that I'm a . . . well as I *did*—it came slowly through the college years and the . . . well, it's still going on . . . the business of finding out what it is that I really want which means, you know, what I really am, and in my case just through the years sort of developing slowly, more and more courage. . . . I'm not fully courageous yet, you might say because as I work I have things now which are safe in the privacy of my journal.

Frick: Things you haven't committed yet?

Maslow: No, they're so far out, they're so. . . . I still get nightmares a little bit before I'll publish it.

Frick: . . . even with your reputation, you still have this kind of inhibition?

Maslow: Well, the reputation is based on something else and this new thing that I want to talk about will offend the people who . . . it will offend my reputation you might say.

Frick: Yes, but you're moving from a position of strength here, you know.

Maslow: Well, I feel more confident—much more than I used to

hen I'd go into prostration. The first talk I gave on the peak expe-
ences and this B-cognition stuff, there was my old professor sitting
 the front row and, God, I couldn't sleep for several nights before-
ind, and I had to rest in fatigue—just exhaustion before and after—
d I had dreams about being thrown out of my family. I remember
ie dream that happened about then. It was sort of a recurrent
·eam whenever I'd say something publicly that had been worked
it privately. It was a typical dream and it sums up this whole
ourage and fear thing—of being in the street and then somebody
·lls, "Hey, lions and tigers are loose," and then I would get fright-
ied and run to the door behind which is my family—not the blood
mily but somehow the whole clan—and bang on the door, crying
et me in, let me in!" And the door is locked, and they don't let me
, and it was definitely the American Psychological Association. I
as always figuring, "My God, they're going to throw me out!" or
'll be cast out," and this, I think, may be a universal fear. If you
y something that contradicts the people you've admired and
arned from, something that contradicts your teachers, this is kind
 a cosmic, eternal thing.

·ick: . . . yes, and whose admiration of you often depends upon
·rtain known positions . . .

aslow: . . . and each time giving up the admiration and in effect
ving up the reputation.

·ick: Right, or running that risk, at least.

aslow: Well, each time unconsciously, I was giving it up.

·ick: That's right. Well, perhaps we should get back to this is-
·e of choice which is very complicated, really. It's a two-fold kind
 thing; choosing to recognize and go into your uniqueness in a
nse, and also choosing to actualize those instinctoid potentials as
·ll.

aslow: That's the same thing.

·ick: Yes, but one is a racial kind of thing as you talk about spe-
·es-wide potentials. The other is more personal and unique in a
nse but they're not mutually exclusive.

Maslow: Well, that's one of the things that I'm trying to do, to
·rk very, very carefully to select the words so that they're just

right. The word I'd use there would be not uniqueness. I'd u
rather "idiosyncratic" meaning individual. That is, the way
which we're different from other people is also discovered in th
same personal, self-searching indentity-seeking kind of thing.

Frick: In the instinctoid base?

Maslow: That's right. But that which is not unique to me, b
which we all share I discover by the same process; that is, in dept
in psychoanalysis let's say, I will discover as a great discovery t
need for love, which I share with everybody, and the process itsel
that is, the discovering of what's common to the species, and wh
is unique to me—comes after the fact of discovery and uncovering

Frick: Yes. Right.

Maslow: At least, that's the way I would say it to save the uniqu
ness and idiosyncratic qualities and their difference from speci
wide things, and yet also to save this similarity process by which v
discover ourselves. Subjectively my need for safety, or my tenden
to express my ectomorphic rather than mesomorphic type of i
telligence are discovered in . . . and then let's say my malene
which is not species-wide and then even more let's say, my partic
lar level of intelligence and my particular yearnings, let's say, fo
good world, etc., that these are discovered the same way. All of t
species-wide, half species-wide, big groups, and then finally the i
osyncratic.

Frick: You don't think then, Dr. Maslow, that you are returning
a kind of an instinct psychology as we used to know it?

Maslow: No, no. I reject the MacDougal theory as I do the etholc
ist's instinct theory since it just doesn't apply. It's essentially beha
ioral theory and I'm not talking about behavior. The behavic
which are genetically determined are so trivial, not trivial but r
flex, that they just don't matter for the psychologist much. I'm tal
ing rather about impulses or even better said, I am referring
needs in the strict sense. Needs for the sake of physical health a
full humanness.

Frick: Right. Dr. Maslow, I think you have been criticized . . .

Maslow: . . . I could be criticized for using that word "instinctoic
because it has brought misunderstanding, but I just couldn't thi

any other word. And that, too, is blunt. It joins the issue sharply, ιd I keep getting impatient with the sociologizing and the envi-ιnmentalizing of psychology, and of making principles which ap-ly to *any* species and which are not species-specific to the human ιecies. So that word is . . . I'd apologize for it on the one hand be-ιuse it does mislead more than I expected. On the other hand you ιve to have something like that because the issue is fudged too of-ιn. It gets involved with your politics, too. Erich Fromm, for in-ιance, is just ducking the issue, really, even though he says it in a ιlf dozen indirect ways.

rick: He takes a very similar position, doesn't he?

Maslow: Well, without saying so. I think it *is* a similar position. I ιink that Carl Rogers takes a similar position but one time when ·e were sort of debating (at the University of Florida, I think), I ιose this one issue as *the* one difference of opinion, and then Carl ιid, "Well, I don't disagree." And I said, "Well, say so." And he ιd. And yet there is something not quite respectable about using ιrtain words.

rick: It's been contaminated, hasn't it, by MacDougal and all of ιe instinct people, and it's hard to return to in any way, I think.

Dr. Maslow, you've been criticized for your emphasis on the goal f becoming fully human, becoming everything the person can be-ιme. Now, some have said that you're very indiscriminate here, ιat you see this in kind of an unrealistic global fashion. My ques-ion is, doesn't the person have to make choices and select from a ·emendous reservoir of potentials and must there not be some pri-rity in terms of what the person sets out to really actualize within ιmself? You wouldn't disagree with this, would you?

Maslow: Absolutely not. But again it's very hard to find the words. ·he only way you can say this is in extenso with lots of examples. ιou can't make a neat and simple statement about it. Of course I gree. I hope to do a systematic book if I live long enough, present-ιg a thorough system of human nature. I hope to expand the last ιhapter in my *Toward a Psychology of Being,* called "Some Basic ιropositions of a Growth and Self-Actualizing Psychology" and de-ιelop a comprehensive philosophy of psychology, and I hope to ex-ιnd that material into seventeen volumes or so.

Frick: . . . magnificent!

Maslow: Well, do the old German professor, 19th Century Hand
buch in seven volumes, you know.

Frick: Are you timid about this:

Maslow: No.

Frick: . . . as you think about it?

Maslow: No. That I enjoy. As a matter of fact, that is . . . that's
timidity chasing thing, because that would be systematic. It's no
trying to say in a brief span something which cannot be said in
brief span. That will give me the extensiveness that I want, so the
I can address myself to all these questions that you have raised.

Frick: Then you can take care of all of these discrepancies.

Maslow: Absolutely and really get the thousands of footnotes an
the data. I have a form that I'm putting this in—my death-defyin
form, I call it—which will grow biologically, sort of by i
tussusception which is the way we grow rather than the way a pil
of stones does. It will grow from within as we do, keeping the sam
proportions. I have about 200 propositions, and I can make kind c
a brief statement about them in a page, or two or three. Then I'
have for each of those, an appendix containing the supportive dat
and with reference also to the data which we do not yet have—all c
the experiments I'd love to do if we had a 200-year life span.

Frick: It would certainly encourage further research, thougl
wouldn't it?

Maslow: That's what I want to do, that's what I'd like to do. I'
probably end my life with that because that can be published th
day after I die. It will be in shape so that it is always completec
And yet it can grow.

Frick: Right.

Maslow: And if I live to the age of 80, then it is going to be an aw
fully big book.

                    ☼   ☼   ☼   ☼   ☼

Frick: Dr. Maslow, with your concern for developing the huma
potential you would say, then, that a very narrow person, focusin

on model train building, for example, let's say this is his real "thing." This is how he expresses and finds himself. If he were that narrow, that is, if this was his consuming interest could this person be self-actualizing?

Maslow: Well, let's take a better example, because probably that would be neurotic, that is, if you poked into such a person you'd find that this was a flight from or a defense against something. That's just sort of my expectation—it might be wrong—this might be full self-actualizing for, let's say, an un-intelligent person. That might be the best he can do.

Frick: It would be consistent with his other potentials, then?

Maslow: Well, I think we get . . . for instance, I find myself getting narrow, oh, more and more narrow with my age and becoming so absorbed in my work that I've given up plays, and poetry and making new friends, which I just don't do anymore.

Frick: . . . you say you have given all of these things up?

Maslow: Yes. I love my work so much, and am so absorbed with it, that everything else starts getting to look smaller and smaller.

Frick: Is this good? Is this self-actualizing?

Maslow: Well, whatever it is, I'm doing it. I don't know. We just don't know.

Frick: It's hard to judge, isn't it? This is what we're saying, and this is kind of what I was asking here.

Maslow: Well, I ran across this statement in Darwin. Darwin, saying something of the sort, said he finally turned into what he thought was a dry, narrow man, just absorbed with his work, and with nothing else in the whole world. If I compared this with the reading of novels, and going on trips, and going to parties, and doing a thousand things, all of which I enjoy doing—I hardly listen to my records anymore, except for background things. I am so much more narrowed down to my work which I think is more and more me and more and more what's important.

Frick: All right, you're making choices, aren't you? This is self-actualizing for you, although you are making certain sacrifices as well.

Maslow: Yes. Whether that's a good thing or a bad thing, I don't know. For society I suspect it's a good thing.

Frick: For you as a person it may be limiting.

Maslow: Yes. I feel sad over . . .

Frick: . . . what you're missing in other ways?

Maslow: Yes, I . . . all the pleasures that I . . . This semester, for instance, I gave up the Audubon walks in the woods, and the bird walks, which I love. Well, it just took too much time. Well, what did it take time from? I loved it, and yet sacrificed, renounced it, gave it up for the sake of my mission, or vocation, or calling, or something.[1]

Frick: Now, I would like to ask something here, Dr. Maslow. It seems to me that . . . Rollo May has made this point, and I think you have, too, although I'm not sure I could locate it right now, but I am referring to the need in creative work to have these moments of self-renewal, to have the passive moments—the bird walks, and so forth—and I'm wondering what your sacrifice is in terms of giving up a lot of moments of serenity and peace and calm, and these other interests. Would they not feed back into your work in a very stimulating way?

Maslow: Yes, they do, and I do walk a lot—anyway I must for health reasons. And yet somehow I feel better about the walks, you know, it isn't just a waste of time because I can meditate on the work I am doing, and other things I am thinking about. But it's a little . . . it's very hard to describe, because rather a few people have that sense of mission. I know Rollo May does have it. Rollo May is a world savior, too. The way I'd say it for myself, and I've said it to other people to try to explain and to my wife, for instance, when I don't go to the play with her and try to justify myself. Supposing you found a cure for cancer, what would *you* do? Could you then go to the theater and sit and watch the play?

Frick: When work has to be done . . .

---

[1] In interpreting Dr. Maslow's increasing devotion to his work, it should be stressed that he had had a heart attack prior to this interview. The insecurity over his health undoubtedly played some part in his growing sense of commitment.

Maslow: Yes, when work has to be done, and mankind has to be helped. This is the way I feel, although it's really more important than cancer. How can I piddle around at these things and yet it's an overstatement because, well, I went to a party last night. It was our department party and I enjoy parties, yet I think I am just most happy and most fulfilled, and most myself, and most being as if that's what I were meant to be when I am involved in my work.

Frick: A mission is a good word for it, isn't it? A sense of mission.

Maslow: There are the old words for it. You find your vocation, or your calling.

Frick: Sidney Jourard has called it your "project." There are many words for it.

    ✿   ✿   ✿   ✿   ✿

Frick: Viktor Frankl, as you know, has been critical of you, Dr. Maslow, in his article "Beyond Self-Actualization and Self-Expression." I think you had a rebuttal or a rejoinder to that article but I didn't read it. Frankl says that you have . . . or the self-actualizing psychologists have neglected "that sphere of human existence in which man chooses what he will do, and what he will be in the midst of an objective world of meanings and values."[2] Now, in the light of what we have already talked about, would you say that Frankl really didn't understand your position here? Because it seems to me you're not denying the importance of choice.

Maslow: Well, we got together on that like two co-workers and straightened it out and agreed and he felt quite good about that. My article wasn't a rebuttal, exactly, but sort of an explanation and a sharpening up, underscoring, and the like. And we certainly agree on that. I think he must be pleased with the paper with which I really finished a 25 year project . . . I finished the paper and then I had a heart attack, and it's as if it were a . . . I had been staggering along working so hard, and that was my job, that was the end. Then I had the sense of completion with this theory of metamotivation. Did I send you a copy of that?

---

[2] Viktor Frankl, "Beyond Self-Actualization and Self-Expression," *Journal of Existential Psychiatry* Vol. 1, No. 1 (Spring 1960, [5–20]): p. 17.

Frick: Yes, and it was also published in the *Journal of Humanistic Psychology,* I believe, more recently.[3]

Maslow: Yes, Well, in this paper I think it is much more worked out and much more detailed along Frankl's line of what *is* the meaning of life, and what are the end goals, and what do you seek what do we all seek, so I feel that there is no real argument between us. He was over at my place, oh, several months ago when he was in the neighborhood, and we talked. I agree with *him,* by the way, just to make it explicit that there is something beyond self-actualization, something beyond the full identity and the real self, and I think I would go much further than Frankl and call it "cosmo-genic," as somebody has called it.

Frick: I'm not sure that Frankl would agree with you that values are instinctoid, would he?

Maslow: We did not discuss that.

Frick: This, I think, is an issue that I see you different on.

Maslow: Well, that might be a struggle over words, and then my guess is again, and I've done this often enough instead of arguing with people, you get together before the fire place with a couple of martinis, and just hash it out.

Frick: You're really saying the same things.

Maslow: Well, we then find the super-ordinate language which we can both utilize.

Frick: The meeting ground, yes.

✿   ✿   ✿   ✿   ✿

Frick: Dr. Maslow, you have characterized self-actualizing people as exemplars, as good choosers, as representing lives that reflect these higher instinctoid values. In other words, you seem to feel as if the people you've studied and whom you've identified as self-actualizing really provide an answer to the question "What is the good life?" You have also suggested that the free choices and the values of the self-actualizing individuals indicate what is good for most other human beings. Now, if this is true, if we find in our research

---

[3] Abraham H. Maslow, "A Theory of Metamotivation: The Biological Rooting of the Value-Life," *Journal of Humanistic Psychology* Vol. VII, No. 2 (Fall, 1967).

that what you say is very definitely true, how would you implement such a finding? What does this mean? I must confess that it frightens me a bit.

Maslow: Well, I would say in the first place, that is very clearly not a factual statement, but an extrapolation or an hypothesis. I just feel that it's probably so but I don't know for sure, and I wish it were possible to have the research institutes to work with such questions. What does self-actualization mean in feeble-minded people? Or what does self-actualization mean and is it possible for somebody caught in a situation where he has to sacrifice his own individual potentials. You know, the man with four kids and a lousy job, and a mortgage. He may know what he wants to do, but for the sake of others cannot do it. Of course, a way of testing the hypothesis is to see how it works. Supposing what I suggest is true, then what happens? Many people are working on these problems and I'm doing it at the theoretical level, but for instance, much of the turmoil that is going on in education now—the new affective education for instance—is based on this assumption and represented by the Esalen approach, or the Summerhill kind of thing, which is really based upon a kind of a trust or a faith that's not a fact yet. I mean it's not proven. Well, let's assume this is true, and then act on that assumption and let's see what happens. Now, acting on that assumption works pretty well in education but not with the establishment education which acts on a different assumption and therefore, I think, is partially a failure, but the assumption is that if you leave people to their own resources, then they will "grow"; if you leave things to individual choice, they will generally, statistically, in the long run choose well rather than badly; if you give freedom, it will be well used if the people are reasonably decent to start with and not too psychopathological. Well, they're using that assumption in many areas. The whole Theory Y management of education is based upon the assumption that human beings seek to actualize a higher nature. Now we are learning about when it works and when it doesn't work and under what circumstances and what the necessary prerequisites are and how to do it, and the strategy and tactics of it, and when it fails and you get the richness of detail, and this is now happening in education, it is also happening in management and organization development. In these two huge areas there is a lot of work going on this assumption and it works out pretty well.

Frick: I was thinking that if you really identified what these instinctoid values were in the human being and you wanted to implement this in terms of an educative process, would this not lead to something very close to behavioral engineering, or would it not lead to something very similar to what Skinner is suggesting? This is what I was wondering about, the problem of implementing these values.

Maslow: Yes, I think I agree with you that it can look like that superficially but, profoundly, it's not like that because this is the difference between control and . . .

Frick: . . . and allowing it to happen . . .

Maslow: That's right, it's the difference between a controlling Frazier as in Walden Two[4]—when a benevolent philosopher-king can, in fact, shape behavior. I have no doubt about it, that whenever we have had a philosopher-king in human history, things went well. The only question is that in Walden Two there are *two* psychologies. There's the psychology of the people, and there's the Frazier psychology. Who picks Frazier? How does he come to pass? How do you not get a Hitler there instead of a Frazier? If you use controlling techniques; controlling, shaping, modeling, molding techniques, then the question comes up of the controller and the shaper or the sculptor. And the other philosophy has had its roots very, very differently because it's more taoistic and receptive and trusting. You don't have to shape human nature, it shapes itself to a much greater extent, I don't know how much yet, but certainly to a greater extent than any other great culture has ever acknowledged. That's one reason I have such great faith in the future of the United States, and of the world, too. I think we're the first culture in history—first large culture—that has built itself pretty firmly on the notion of a higher nature of man and that if you give him the freedom to choose, that he'll choose wisely. You know, the one man-one vote rule is the actualization of that faith; or the free press, or our way of sportsmanship in politics. If you lose an election you just rally behind the man you've just been fighting. This is extremely different from getting a big stork to govern over the frogs and hoping that

---

[4] B. F. Skinner, *Walden Two* (New York: The MacMillan Company, 1948).

you'll get a benevolent one. Now, human history teaches us that most people have not been benevolent when they got power. People who struggle for power, the people who love power are apt to be not benevolent, and the best kind of leader, if you have to have a leader, is one who is a leader very reluctantly. Now it's perfectly true that if I had an ideal school I would use the teaching machines very widely. I think they're very useful, but I think of them in a taoistic way. That is, they're available, like a smorgasbord, for anybody to use if and when he wishes to use it, and to go at his own pace, to be idiosyncratic—that's purely individual—and not one of a class of 35 sitting in rows. Now, if I like teaching machines and Fred Skinner likes teaching machines, it's really a superficial comparison because the philosophy which underlies it is very, very different.

Frick: Yes, very different.

✣ ✣ ✣ ✣ ✣

Dr. Maslow, you have indicated that most people do not know or appreciate their strivings to become more fully human. You have said: "All he knows is that he is dominated by certain needs of the moment. He does not know in advance that he will strive on after this gratification has come, for another higher need. The absolute value for him is the need in the hierarchy he is dominated by during a particular period." I think this appears in your recent book *Toward a Psychology of Being.*[5] Now, my question is: Can human beings be taught to develop an attitude toward themselves that would incorporate a concept of growth and the concept of process toward self-actualization? I think this is crucial here, and I am wondering if you feel this is something we can teach people to feel about themselves, even if they're struggling with a deficiency need.

Maslow: Well, it's happening now, and if I were to re-write that material you just quoted I'd say it in a different way, because the happenings in the last couple of years have been sort of like a huge experiment. My book *Toward a Psychology of Being,* for instance, has been read and sold very widely, and mostly, I gather, among young people. It has sold about 150,000 copies by now, and appar-

---

[5] Abraham Maslow, *Toward a Psychology of Being,* 2nd. Edition (Princeton, N.J.: D. Van Nostrand Company, Inc., 1968).

ently it's been used for helping to produce this kind of insight in hippie groups and among many, many youngsters of the more educated . . . College people, for instance, are setting for themselves these goals in a very conscious way. The goals of authenticity, what we might call idealism. You know, the idealistic goals of these B-values, these ultimate goals of truth and honesty and pure justice and excellence and the renunciation of hypocrisy and phoniness. The kids are doing it. Now, they're doing it stupidly and inefficiently and incapably and they want it *now*.

Frick: . . . . Right, next week at least.

Maslow: And they don't realize that that's a lifetime project and that you struggle and work toward it, and that it doesn't come in a big, single peak experience. Well, in psychoanalytical terms, they're apt to make too great a stress on the *insight* and not enough on the working through. Working through is a lifetime business, and if you want to become a good pianist, or a good anything, you just work.

✓ **Frick:** Self-discipline is something that enters in here that they don't want to accept as part of it, I think.

Maslow: That's right and there was one lapel button I saw that summed it up perfectly—somebody on the West Coast put them out—and it's called "Nirvana, *Now!*" Of course this is something we can learn from, too. If these youngsters that I'm thinking about are very self-consciously seeking for self-actualization and ultimate values, and metamotivations and so on, their goals are wonderful, the goals are fine, but the strategy and tactics are very inefficient.

Frick: Do you feel . . . are you really speaking now of college students who may be struggling at some deficiency-level? Do you feel like they can really develop this orientation to their own growth even when struggling down here at a deficiency level?

Maslow: . . . If they would say it the way you just said it. In my seminars I've been trying the role of the consultant rather than the professor in charge, and what has happened now in two seminars was that when I threw away the reins and abdicated power, then these students spontaneously went into a kind of a T-group situation. That is, what they looked for was belongingness with each other, communication, affection, love, and working together, which is really at a very low level of personal development. This seminar I just had was a kind of a marathon which they did themselves. I was not there. They were in complete charge and they came out with their eyes glowing as people usually do from these things, but this is a re-discovering of the . . . it's a dropping of the defenses, and a re-discovering when it works well, of communion, of belongingness, of love for each other which they've never experienced, and then they take the content and throw it the hell away. They forget about the topic and glory in feeling communion with each other. Then it can make you very sad.[6] My God, they should have had that four or five, or six years ago. Of course this is a much more prepotent need, to communicate with other people and to feel brotherly . . .

Frick: . . . and the cognitive needs somehow . . .

Maslow: Well, they're much less important.

✿ ✿ ✿ ✿ ✿

Frick: Dr. Maslow, in your article on metamotivation which was recently published, you said, "Metamotivation now seems not to ensue automatically after basic-need gratification."[7] Now, it seems to me that this represents an important shift in your theoretical position. Is this true?

Maslow: Yes, it's a surprise. I'd always assumed, the way Freud did—maybe I learned it from Freud—that if you cleared away the rubbish, and the neuroses and the garbage and so on, then the person would blossom out, that he'd find his own way. I find especially with young people that it just ain't so sometimes. You get people who are in the . . . beautiful . . . need-gratifying situation and yet get kind of a value pathology. That is, it's possible to be loved and respected, etc. and even so, to feel cynical and nihilistic, and to feel there's nothing worth working for, which is nonsense, of course. Especially in younger rather than older people, you can see this. It's sort of a loss of nerve, and I think we're at this point where the traditional culture has broken down altogether, and for many people they just feel, "My God, there's nothing."

---

[6] A. H. Maslow, "Humanistic Education vs. Professional Education," *New Directions in Teaching* 2, No. 1 (1969): 6–8.

[7] Abraham Maslow, "A Theory of Metamotivation," *Journal of Humanistic Psychology* Vol. VIII, No. 2 (Fall 1967): p. 94.

Frick: . . . there's nothing else but to be gratified in a sense, and it goes back to Schachtel's concept of imbeddedness,[8] I think, don't you?

Maslow: There's some tendency to regress . . .

Frick: Well, safety, you say, is prepotent. Isn't this involved here?

Maslow: Yes, but I'm talking about people who, as nearly as I can make out, have been brought up well, in my sense, and are living in a very good situation. These *are* the basic-need gratifications so far as safety and security is concerned, and the love and belongingness is concerned. You know, they have enough glory and applause and appreciation, and self respect and yet they look out on the world and on society and say, "My God, what a shambles," and then feel hopeless, some of them.

Frick: In other words, even with all these basic gratifications, they don't move on into any self-actualizing kind of stage?

Maslow: Some do, and some don't. That's quite clear. Some do not. They just get depressed at that point, or a lot of other stuff that I've described as metapathology including value disturbances of all kinds: not only cynicism and nihilism, and sort of a destructive type of anarchism rather than the constructive kind, but anomie and hopelessness and pessimism of a kind that, you know, that produces apathy, and then perfectionism which we've seen in the last election of "either I'll have the perfect way or I won't play the game," which, of course, doesn't fit in the real world. This can happen. It can happen with a fair proportion of the youngsters who drop out of the society, and who move toward death, I think, in many cases.

Frick: And in terms of your hierarchy of needs these young people are basically pretty well gratified, aren't they?

Maslow: That's right, that's right, and this was a surprise. This I've learned really, fully, in the last three or four years.

Frick: What does this mean theoretically, Dr. Maslow? What are the implications here for theory?

Maslow: Well, for me, it makes me feel like more of a missionary than ever. You know, my God, we have that wrong, because there

---

[8] E. G. Schachtel, *Metamorphosis* (New York: Basic Books, 1959).

are values. And then I start thinking about publicity and how to get it around, and you know, communication and printing, and writing and distributing, large mass circulation magazines and stuff like that.

Frick: Well, what are the variables here? Let's say we take two people, and one is very basically need-gratified and feeling safe, secure, comfortable, and operating within this framework. The other person is also equally gratified, and yet one person moves on toward something better, more self-actualizing and another person stays put in an imbedded sense. Now, what makes the difference?

Maslow: Well, that's one of the things I'm working on. I'm now in this stage of trying to work out the vocabulary and to crystallize it in my own thoughts. Broadly, it's pro-life and pro-death. There are many other overlapping terms: the winner and the loser, the striver and the non-striver, the success and the failure type, the weak struggler or the active and passive. This is what I am struggling with right now, to find out how it is that some people find the world is beautiful and worthwhile and other people, if they don't get everything they want, are perfectly willing to die or to say "the hell with the whole damn thing." I've made up all sorts of words, none of them quite good yet, but for the moment, I'm talking about pro-life or life-positive in Wilhelm Reich's sense.

Frick: . . . but this life-positive orientation doesn't necessarily come about automatically, does it, as a function of basic need-gratification? Now where does it come? Where does it enter in?

Maslow: Well, again I think it is constitutional in large part, or it can be constitutional. For instance, I watched my granddaughter, two months old (at 4 A.M.) she's such a . . . well, it could be seen at the age of 24 hours. This was an active baby in the psychoanalytical sense. She was willful. She wanted what she wanted, by gosh. It's not just restlessness. She'll yell her head off until you give her what she wants.

Frick: It's a sense of purpose right there, early.

Maslow: Yes. She needs what she needs when she needs it. She wants what she wants when she wants it, and it's very definite, she knows what she wants. That's another theory: this whole theory of impulse voices—that is of the signal—inner signals. She *knows* when

she's hungry and a passive child or the quiet baby comes into the
world without strong appetites, so that they fall asleep at the breast
in the middle of the feeding, or, and this is a test for passive children, if you take the breast away from them in the middle of the
feeding they're apt to fall asleep, whereas the active baby will yell
his head off in indignation. At the extreme it's as if, I'm taking an
extreme obsessional now, he doesn't really know what's going on at
all inside himself and he lives by external cues all together; the
clock, the calendar, and the schedule. In research work with the
obese people, we have discovered that they don't know when to
stop eating. They don't know when to start eating, either, and they
go by the clock.

Frick: It's time to eat now, kind of thing.

Maslow: That's right, and if you push the clock back, then they eat
some more. The wisdom of the body is less, and I think maybe what
we call life-positive are people with strong appetites. Well, im-
pulse-voices is my word. It's not quite accurate, but in order to
keep your theoretical structure comprehensive something like that
has to fill in the gaps in theory to answer this question which you
raised, which is such an important, crucial question. I wasn't aware
of the *question* until a couple of years ago.

Frick: Dr. Maslow, it seems to me that this calls for a kind of a re-
working of your whole need hierarchy theory somehow. The implications are rather important here and I'm inclined to think that this
is less instinctoid, that is, the moving over the hurdle, after basic
need-gratification I would like to think is less instinctoid than apparently you do.

Maslow: Well, what I'm tentatively thinking and, you know, your
guess is as good as mine. . . . If we had lots of decades more to live,
and to work at it, I would try to test this hypothesis of the impulse
voices, meaning the strength of the need. That is, to save the whole
need hierarchy. There's another variable, maybe, which is the
strength of the whole blasted thing, or the weakness of the whole
thing.

Frick: Right—all the way through. Yes, that would bridge the gap
then, wouldn't it?

Maslow: That's right. The weakly, hungry person, the weakly sexed person, the one who can't sleep—who's not a good sleeper, or the one who's less apt to know what he wants because the voice is so weak.

Frick: Well, you know, certain studies have been made comparing sexual gusto and activity with zest in eating and they seem to go together, this appetite kind of thing.

Maslow: I haven't read any of those studies but I would guess that.

Frick: Dr. Maslow, this seems to suggest that this plateau, or this stage in one's life, is damned important—that is, after the basic needs have been gratified. This seems to be a crucial period for people—in marriage, and personally—do you sense this?

Maslow: Well, I just wrote a paper about it. It's going to be published next year some time and is called "Theory Z," did I send that to you?

Frick: No, I'd like to have it.

Maslow: Then I'll give you a copy of it.

Frick: This may be the most crucial period that man goes through, you know, if we could identify when he goes through it. I think it's different for different people, but . . .

Maslow: Well, we can talk about self-actualizing people at different levels much more than I ever thought ten years ago. For one thing there's this becoming acquainted with people who had everything. I mean everything in my terms, in psychological terms rather than automobiles, and yet who could be quite unhappy and not know their way and stagger, and stumble around and do all sorts of dopey things, and stupid things. Then there was another differentiation that I had to make, that of people who were basic need-gratified, neurosis free, and using some capacitites well and yet being "merely healthy" as I call it, the "merely healthy" as over against the transcenders. Well, I think the difference comes from those who have peak experiences and those who don't, more or less. That's what I described first for self-actualizing people who are transcenders mostly, people in whom the basic need gratification would automatically lead to the value system which implies also the bodhisattva path. That is, the helping service to humanity or the helping of other people.

Frick: The homonomous kind of development.

Maslow: That's right, and of simply becoming better human beings for others, as well as for themselves, and finally of transcending the ego . . .

Frick: . . . in peak experience?

Maslow: That's right, and then of remaining that way, that is, becoming a different kind of human being in the Eastern sense, or the awakened, or the illuminated, or what we might call the "sage," or what I prefer to call the sage-saint. Well, the one who really got me onto this distinction was Eleanor Roosevelt who just had no peak experiences. She said she didn't know what it meant and yet she was clearly self-actualizing by all the criteria I had set forth: she was basic need-gratified, using capacities well, using herself well, obviously not a neurotic person, and she had transcended the troubles of her childhood.

Frick: . . . and yet something was missing.

Maslow: Something was missing and then I got pushed into the corner with this. Then I had to say . . . well, take a man like Truman, who is clearly not a lofty person, not a saint, you could hardly call him that—or even a sage—or finally, just to make it, with Eisenhower. I just can't have great respect for him, but he fits our criteria, at least these minimal criteria, and so then I talk about the "merely healthy." I called it at first the "Truman-Eisenhower-Roosevelt" syndrome and separated it off from people like Martin Buber and Aldous Huxley whom I worked with before he died, and people like that. Well, these were two trends of people. With Truman and Eisenhower you can talk about values and there is apt to be an acceptance of the culture. They like the culture and they find it quite good, and work within it, and improve within it. Certainly their aims are benevolent, they're well wishers, and they have no malice. Eisenhower certainly has very little malice. He's a nice man, and a good man *but* something is missing. And so I talk about "merely healthy" then. This last paper, I think, is very important for me, because I have to struggle through with these issues. You are raising questions which I have to raise and which were very disturbing and confusing.

　　　　✿　　✿　　✿　　✿　　✿

Frick: Dr. Maslow, some good material has been written recently concerning crisis theory. This is something I'm particularly interested in at the present time and I wonder what you think of it, and in the light of our conversation whether this may be one possible answer to explain what can happen to help individuals move from basic need-gratification or the "merely healthy" level into true self-actualization. Now, I'm thinking of Dabrowski's book, *Positive Disintegration.*[9] I'm thinking of Ronald Laing's center for so-called psychotics and also of Menninger's recent attention to this issue in his book *The Vital Balance.*[10] In a provocative section he calls "weller than well" Menninger talks about the tremendous potential of crisis and disintegration for the personality in terms of personality growth. Now, maybe here is a possible answer for a lot of people. In other words, the men I have mentioned see crisis and disintegration of the personality as a prerequisite for growth at different periods of time in life. What do you think about this?

Maslow: Well, it looks as if it is more true than otherwise. I can certify it's not always true. There are people who are very fortunate people, and I just have no idea of their number in the population, but there are some people who just placidly and calmly live a good life without great crisis, that is, without disintegration.

Frick: But are they "merely healthy?"

Maslow: No, they can move on to the highest levels that we know about.

Frick: . . . and do it gradually?

Maslow: . . . and do it gradually. I think they're probably less in number than the ones who have to go into a big turmoil to come through to . . .

Frick: . . . higher levels of integration.

Maslow: Yes, but as to the Dabrowski theory, I have a pal that I work with, a psychoanalyst, and we've published a paper together

---

[9] Kazimierz Dabrowski, *Positive Disintegration* (Boston: Little, Brown and Company, 1964).
[10] Karl Menninger, *The Vital Balance* (New York: The Viking Press, 1963). See pages 406–417.

and probably will others.[11] He's a good friend, and I like talking with him. He gives me my vicarious clinical experience which I don't have the time for now, and we've talked for about ten years. He had a patient about ten years ago who was almost a model for the crisis theory, maybe better than some of Dabrowski's cases. Here was a guy who was a patient and he was a patient for being a son-of-a-bitch, to put it briefly. He was a nasty man. He was very wealthy and used people, especially women, and he was sadistic and cruel. In psychoanalysis things moved a little too fast, I would guess, and he realized he was a son-of-a-bitch. I think this was just too much for a person to take, and he went crazy. He went into a florid psychosis, a schizophrenic psychosis, and was in the hospital for about eight months. But somehow, perhaps because he was in psychoanalysis through it all, he retained all the insights that a schizophrenic can have and he came out a wonderful man. He came out a very fine man who devoted himself to good works.

Frick: A complete switch of the value system.

Maslow: Absolutely, and he has been that way ever since, about ten years. He never will have another psychotic break. There's no doubt about it.

Frick: That's quite a story.

Maslow: We've watched him, and followed this up through the years and you would say now, "He's a very fine man."

Frick: Has this been written up at all?

Maslow: I think I mentioned it in some place, but we had thought to get more cases, but they just never came along in that same beautiful way. Also my impulse is that if somebody else is doing it, well, they're taking care of it. Dr. Hobart Mowrer has been collecting such cases for about a decade and the conversion experience which is part of it. Silverman, Grof, Laing, and Dabrowski are using disintegration—these sudden breaks—and using it well for insight and then for working through. In just the same way that you would say with LSD, it can be either a plain kind of damaging thing, or if it's used well, then it can help, and it can be built upon and of

---

[11] Dr. Harry Rand, psychoanalyst.

course, Dabrowski is building upon it. Only this does not always happen. In getting the life history of a group of self-actualizing people I discovered that two of them were severely neurotic, characteristically into their 40's. Then there was a great cosmic consciousness, a sort of a conversion moment. In one of the persons it was *a* single moment where he saw the whole world differently. I don't know whether to call it a peak experience or not. I call it cosmic consciousness following Bucke.[12] In the other person it took about a week. It was a week of turmoil and of change but in essence a sort of cosmic consciousness. And the neuroses disappeared, spontaneously, forever, and then they became what I saw, these wonderful people, saintly people. So this can happen, there's no question about it.

Frick: Yes, and you're suggesting here that the crisis experience is most valuable for a person who has been living a neurotic or disturbed life up to that point, aren't you?

Maslow: Well, I would say . . . my guess is that if the life were too neurotic, there would be a very severe break.

Frick: . . . there would have to be, to change.

Maslow: That's right, and I think that throughout history they would have simply gone crazy, and stayed crazy. Now we have new knowledge, new techniques.

Frick: Now we have a different way of looking at the experience, don't we?

Maslow: That's right, that's right.

Frick: Laing sees it, for example, as a voyage into the self, a self-discovery kind of voyage, and it's quite a unique way of looking at the psychoses, I think.

Maslow: Well, the man who taught *me* that . . . as much as anyone else, was well . . . this case . . . this one case of my friend I have already mentioned. John Rosen's understanding of schizophrenia was for me very helpful. I think I got more feeling, more instruction out of Hannah Green's book, *I Never Promised You a Rose Garden*,[13]

---

[12] R. M. Bucke, *Cosmic Consciousness* (Philadelphia: Innes and Sons, 1901).
[13] Hannah Green, *I Never Promised You a Rose Garden* (New York: Holt, Rinehart and Winston, 1964).

than I have out of any book I've ever read on schizophrenia. That's a wonderful book and I've used it for my students.

Frick: It is a beautiful thing.

Maslow: I'm not going in much for crisis theory because other people are taking care of it very nicely, and I would add there the Erik Erikson kind of thing,[14] the milder or the normal crisis, you might say.

Frick: I do a lot of counseling work at Albion College and I experienced the value of crisis even before I was very familiar with crisis theory. I was having experiences with students in therapy over and over again that bore this out. I had a dramatic one early this semester, extremely dramatic, and it was the same kind of thing.

Maslow: Well, you keep your eye open, and you will find among your best people . . . I'm thinking now of one girl, who may be certainly one of the best in the psychological sense. She was a wonderful young woman, whom I knew first as a freshman, about eight years ago. The critical moments or the crises for her were mild. They weren't great blowups. She had a wonderful father whom I had met and talked with, and she's just lived a good life. She's a strong girl and was able. . . . Every crisis she ever went through was so fruitful for her that it was mild, you might say. The Laing model really is too extreme. She lived a good life, just as if she were going step by step upward, without any steps back.

Frick: She was able to make use of these experiences on her own, maybe, without a lot of help.

Maslow: Well, some help. I was the benevolent one around because I liked her and I was so interested in her; then her father must have been a help because he was a very fine, understanding man. But essentially she was on her own, and she handled herself very, very well.

Frick: Dr. Maslow, our discussion of crisis theory leads me into another question. You've talked about the perfect society and have used the concept of synergy.[15] Let us suppose that we could de-

---

[14] See Erik H. Erikson, *Identity: Youth and Crisis* (New York: W. W. Norton and Co., 1968).

velop a healthy or utopian society, compatible with man's intrinsic nature, where we have a synergic relationship between the social system and the individual. What would happen in a society that offered only gratification? Is it possible to conceive of this?

Maslow: Well, we can't conceive of it historically. It's impossible to conceive of, because there is more than just one person. We would have to have conflict and the pacing, at least, of gratification. You'd have to have certain controls, such as inhibitions and delay. I'm talking about Apollonian control as over against repressive control. The Apollonian approach would not call the gratifications into question, but only the pacing and would say, if you Apollonize, "Take it easy, be orderly about this thing and don't rush it." It would actually increase the pleasures of gratification in the long run. But, always there remains the ultimate things of "I fall in love with you, and you know you're not in love with me" or "You're my Papa, and you die, and I'm four years old," etc. I simply cannot conceive of the vicissitudes of life just disappearing, so that we'll always have them. I think that what we'll have to do in the theory of eupsychia is to learn how to make hay out of them, how to use them well, and to learn how to soften the blows when they tend to become traumatic or dangerous. How do we strengthen people so that they can take a trauma and profit by it instead of being hurt by it? I have a big chapter planned in this big system book on the beauties and the benefits of frustration. This is like the Outward Bound kind of thing, do you know what that is? The Outward Bound program is the teaching of young men to handle danger and hardship. You know, the experience of being alone in the wilderness for five days, etc. I think this is very fine and very good for building a stronger person who can then face traumatic experiences and conflicts, and anxieties and overcome them and profit by them.

       ✧   ✧   ✧   ✧   ✧

Frick: Dr. Maslow, There are many fads that have come along as a part of the new third force psychology: sensory awareness, sensitivity groups, nude therapy, and so on. Now, I'm not demeaning these developments, but some of the experiments and activities

---

[15] A. H. Maslow, "Synergy in the Society and in the Individual," *Journal of Individual Psychology* 20 (November 1964).

seem to be peripheral in a sense, and I'm wondering how you look upon them. Are they of real significance in this whole movement?

Maslow: Well, since I've had something to do with all of them, kind of setting them in motion . . . I'm all for . . . I think of this as part of the scientific process. I call it first-stage science. Some people call it openness, being ready to try anything out, but without a priori commitments. That is you try it out the way you try this pair of shoes or another pair of shoes to see how it works, and how it fits, and whether you like it or not. For instance, I had suggested this nude therapy thing in my journal which was published, there was a little suggestion about it and then some guy came along and took it up.

Frick: Paul Bindrim.

Maslow: Yes. I don't think I would have. I think that the culture was not quite ready for it yet. But in principle I'd say, well, because I got involved in it, I would say "Gosh, I don't know how it's going to work. It's a thought, it's an experiment, it's a gamble." Obviously, the thing to do is to try it out, evaluate it and if it works well, then you go on from there. If it works badly then it's out. So that I have no commitment to it working or not working, and I've suggested many things even where I feel skeptical. I think I would gamble that they would *not* work, but I think they ought to be tried anyhow. I think that at this level of scientific exploration we ought to be quite willing to try all sorts of cockeyed experiments and not pre-judge the case. We ought to *post-judge* the case.

Frick: Right, give it a try and then evaluate it.

Maslow: As for fads, anything can become a fad and I, myself, certainly am prepared for that. I mean the history of religions, you know, I was just reading last night about Buddhism and you get a fine man like Buddha and look what happened to his teachings. That's for any religious leader and I think for any intellectual leader, it gets corrupted to some extent, and that's always been true.

Frick: Dr. Maslow, one final question. What do you see for American psychology in the next few decades? What do you see in terms of the status of behaviorism and its future? Where are we going with the new third force psychology? Could you comment briefly on these related items?

Maslow: Well, I'm very convinced that many of our differences in opinions and philosophy are characterological differences and temperamental differences, so I think we are going to have more positivistic people and more humanistic people. I think a million years from today there are going to be people who like rigor more, and those who like rigor less, and people who will like a third decimal place and others who are more global, and some who love warm human relations, and some who love cool human relations. So I think there will always be something of that, and that will have its effects, but I think that for the immediate future we can incorporate. These are not contradictory, except as images of man.

Frick: This is a pretty basic difference, isn't it?

Maslow: They're philosophical differences rather than scientific differences, and I think the philosophical differences are going to become very clear in the next decade.

Frick: A sharpening up of these differences?

Maslow: Yes, so that they won't . . . I think the brightest and most intelligent behaviorists will be content to give up the cosmic kind of generalizations, and to recognize that their work with the pigeons or white rats or whatever is perfectly all right without making a cosmic philosophy out of it. I think we are going to have a much more eclectic psychology or what used to be called eclectic, but I would say now a really more comprehensive philosophy of psychology.

Frick: This is what you're trying to do in your book?

Maslow: That's what I'll be doing if I live long enough. Big job!

Frick: Thank you, Dr. Maslow.

2

Interview with
Dr. Gardner Murphy

George Washington University, February 14, 1969

Frick: Dr. Murphy, as I have studied the holistic personality theorists, I have identified at least two major holistic themes. The first theme stresses the drive for self-consistency, or organization, and bringing completion to incomplete structure. The second theme stresses the evolution of the personality, seeing the personality as always in flux, always growing, changing, and in process. And it seems to me that these two theories of growth are in conflict. If number one is true, that is, if the personality is always striving for organization and cohesion or self-consistency as Lecky called it, what explains growth in the personality and change, and evolution? It seems to me that these two themes have not been adequately tied together theoretically or conceptually, and I wonder if you would comment on this.

Murphy: Well, I think there are two possible answers to that dilemma or apparent contradiction, and the first is represented by Kurt Goldstein going way back to the Gelb-Goldstein studies of brain-injured men in the first World War, showing that visual space, for example, reconstitutes itself after damage to the brain, and the man moves towards an orderly structured, or integrated visual totality. Of course, later, in the other publications like *Human Nature in the Light of Psychopathology,* [1] he developed this into a personality theory, undertaking to show that there is always movement towards the realization of a hidden potential, a somewhat Aristotelian way of viewing growth and assuming that there has to be a final or ultimate goal towards which we move. Now, the other point of view would be represented, I suppose, by orthodox

---

[1] Kurt Goldstein, *Human Nature in the Light of Psychopathology* (New York: Schocken Books, 1963).

‚estalt psychology, let's say by Wertheimer and certainly by Koffka and Köhler, with an emphasis upon movement towards fulfillment of a praegnanz, the achievement of an order which is as good as possible in terms of some logical or mathematical or frankly normative goal of beauty or goodness.

Frick: It's kind of a perfection, isn't it, the striving for an achievement of perfection.

Murphy: Yes, it certainly involves that assumption. If you pursue either of these, either the Goldstein or the classical Gestalt view, you can say that growth of any sort—let's say involving differentiation and then integration of the differentiated parts—is compatible with, or even very close to, this idea of fulfillment. I don't think that the conflict is very great, really, as you state it. I think that there is a potential conflict in the sense that the latter, the evolutionary conception, is closer to data. It's better grounded in observational reality whereas the former as a perfectionist scheme is a Platonic definition of an ideal and, in fact, somewhat glories in its remoteness from empirical grounding. It's for this reason that I have almost no use for the first idea. I have the feeling that most of our contemporary theories of holism are wildly idealistically remote from the grubby difficult task of finding out where growth of a particular sort is actually occurring. I think there's a danger of using fiat, or using verbal violence on the data, to say no matter what disturbed or frightened child you encounter in clinical practice that he is seeking growth. Well, maybe he is seeking to get even with a sibling, or with a father, and all that is immediately apparent is the struggle to inch up a little bit of gamesmanship—one upmanship—in favor of himself at the moment. I think Lecky very grossly ignored that problem in the sense that he actually didn't deal with the fact that a great many people move *away* from consistency with a great deal of satisfaction. They don't want to be trapped into the kind of consistency that . . .

Frick: . . . that he was speaking about.

Murphy: Yes, I think it's the empirical reality that human life is full of both a movement toward consistency and movement away from consistency, at different times, and at different places, with different people. And I think that lacquering this all over with a ort of smooth surface to give the impression that there is only one motive, and that it is in an ideal direction is really a disservice to the investigator's task. Now, I've taken quite a different direction, actually, about this in my efforts to bring Pythagoras into the picture in the little paperback, *Psychological Thought from Pythagoras to Freud*,[2] which was recently published. I have attempted to show that there *is* a kind of perfection in mathematical order as Pythagoras saw it, and as Descartes saw it, and as a number of evolutionary biologists like D'Arcy Thompson are saying it in this century. But I think that that is based on quite firm and solid biological observation and that it remains for the psychologist to show the same degree of discipline, the same respect for data that those biologists have shown. And if they can, in other words, if these ideas about achieving symmetry, rhythm, order, and ultimate perfection are found as richly in psychological domains, particularly in personality study, as they are at the level of studying, let's say, the veins of leaves or the paths of paramesium; if, in other words, psychology can really learn its lesson from biology, then I say we will have gained a great deal from it. I think beginning with the ideal and insisting that our data must take this ideal form is not very helpful in scientific enterprise.

Frick: Well, Dr. Murphy, you're suggesting then that growth and change and the vicissitudes of life that go along with this, is a more important principle than the principle of self-consistency?

Murphy: Yes, I think so, definitely, partly because there are workmanlike, orderly, disciplined ways of approaching problems of growth, rhythm, and symmetry. The techniques have developed to high pitch and need to be respected and used, rather than replaced, I think, by a verbal solution to the problems.

Frick: Dr. Murphy, I had thought that one of the best ways to resolve this conflict, if indeed there is one here between these two principles of growth—consistency versus change—is by using the concept of crisis as a conceptual bridge. That is, it seems to me that if the personality does reach a point of cohesion and self-consistency and stability, the continued growth of that person might be

---

[2] Gardner Murphy, *Psychological Thought from Pythagoras to Freud* (New York: Harcourt, Brace & World, Inc., 1968).

explained by a crisis experience as suggested by Dabrowski in hi.
book *Positive Disintegration,* and in Menninger's *The Vital Balance*
where he talks about people who have grown through crisis. I'n
wondering how you feel about this use of the concept of crisis.

Murphy: Well, I have a great deal of respect for the concept.
would add, I think, reference to the evolutionary sequence of crisi.
as developed, for example in Schrödinger's *What is Life?,* a ver\
brilliant and powerful study, I think, of the way in which "ste\
functions" as he calls them, those sudden, dramatic, forward move
ments that appear in the evolutionary sequence indicating tha
very often, if the organism is stymied for a very long time, it's per
fectly hopeless to expect a series of minimal gradations, like the ol
Darwinian minimal random variations, to produce the new. Yo\
have mutation theory and then you have this theory of the step
function. Now, offering a crisis serves as an alternative way of de
veloping out of the groove in which one has been moving. Anothe
illustration coming from a very different point is Toynbee's idea o
challenge and response, in which he's saying that society may go on fo
thousands of years with very little change, and then may be eithe
made or broken, depending upon the form and amount of challeng
to the traditional ways. The crisis may be sufficiently severe to de
stroy, but if it does not destroy, it may evoke some potential. . . .

Frick: Creating new developments—positive developments.

Murphy: Yes, particularly in the form of leadership. I think Marga
ret Mead's recent book on her follow-up on the Manus study tha
she did in the late 20's, showing the powerful effect of one brilliar
political leader—social, cultural leader—is very interesting in con
trast to the many other hapless groups in the South Pacific tha
didn't have any dramatic leader of the particular sort. I think you
idea also could be pursued in the philosophical direction by goin
back to Hegel and Marx and perhaps Herbert Spencer and in mod
ern times, Heinz Werner, all of whom look for specific dramati
conditions under which a process which is organized at a rather lo\
level is forced by the crisis situation to a higher order and more ar
ticulate form of organization, which is, of course, Herbert Spencer'
idea. But I'm thinking now, particularly, of the dialectical way c
stating this issue as Hegel and then Marx formulated it. I think yo\
can say that we *don't* have a very clear theory of *crisis,* but if yo\

mean a threat to life, if you mean a threat to integrity, then I think the issue can be phrased rather simply as a question of whether there is a tightening of structure, or whether there is a dissolution of structure. You can strike with a battle axe hard enough to crush. Short of that you may just blunt your axe on the metal in the door. It takes a certain intensity to get a result, and of course, biologists are in close touch with this all the time with acid-base balances, and saying that you will get a result, or you will not get a result, depending upon the resistance of the organism to this particular blow that's being applied. Very often you make or break with a single confrontation. I think crisis theory is sound in those cases.

Frick: Dr. Murphy, this leads me to think of the student revolts taking place all over the country today. I was reading the *Washington Post* this morning, and there were about four or five major confrontations going on in institutions across the country yesterday. How do you feel about these student demonstrations and revolts? Doesn't this represent a kind of crisis situation that may evolve into something better for education in the long run? I can't believe it is all bad, although it looks awfully violent right now. I wonder how you view this, and . . .

Murphy: Well, it's a very mixed dish. I don't really know too much about it. My wife and I were teaching in New York City thirty years ago and in that area we saw a great deal of constructive student demand upon faculties. At Sarah Lawrence College where she taught it was very rich in faculty-student channels of communication. Student's ideas were taken very seriously and the progressive achievement of the college was based *largely* upon the willingness of the faculty to listen long and hard to the ideas that were being developed by the students, not only by seniors but even by lower classmen. We didn't get at Columbia as much dialogue as we would have liked. We didn't get as much urgency, as much eagerness on the part of undergraduate students as we could have used. Well, now, we look back at New York after these years and we see a situation—let's begin with Columbia—in which obviously the administration, and to some degree the faculty, had not been distinguished at all for eagerness in getting the student point of view. And when you hear about reports lying on tables for months, you have to ask yourself, "Did the students have reason to believe that they could get a result, except by being pretty vigorous?" And, of course, they went wild. When you start swinging brickbats around, somebody is going to get hurt. Of course, the method is out of proportion. That would follow from the dialectical nature of the discussion: the thesis-antithesis, the "hit-him-once and he-hits-you-twice" kind of approach which is going to be followed when feelings really run high. Now, I don't think that the feelings ran at any time to a point which warrants the feeling on the part of the staff that students have gotten out of hand. They have gotten out of *our* hands, yes, but society is going to be the ultimate judge in this situation through political and economic and other constraints. I don't see how either a public or a private institution of education, and through its administration or its faculty, can take the position that "we know what's good education and we know who should be admitted to this and how he should be guided through the educational process." It seems to me we have discovered collectively as a society that we are not giving an intimate enough, rich enough, individualized enough education. We live in a period of specialization and we don't know how to produce people with broad and general knowledge and wisdom. We know how to make people more and more refined in their specialization. We know how to get government contracts for bigshot professors and to assign graduate students to work with them but we don't really know very much about general education in a free society, as they called it at Harvard. And I think there is going to be a lot of wastage and a lot of skulls are ultimately going to get cracked in the process of adjusting educational systems to the demands of a rapidly changing society.

Frick: . . . and to the needs of the young people as they seem to feel them.

Murphy: I'm putting it that way but I'm putting it, really, primarily in terms of the salvaging of the society in view of the racial tensions, and particularly the international situation and the very considerable likelihood that we will blow ourselves off the face of this earth within a few years at the rate at which things are going. We live with the fail-safe type of risk, and the likelihood of somebody making a blunder somewhere, somehow; the likelihood that the political machinery will become ineffective to control the military potential. It seems to me entirely proper to have a great deal of milling around and experimental efforts to dislodge the present, rather sleepy leadership and get into serious experimentation with our educational system. I think there has been relatively little experimental education in the last few decades. Mostly, people learn their subject-matter stuff and they go into classes and they retell the stuff, and the students write it down, and they go along and find their slots in life, and I don't think that's enough. I don't think that can be justified in terms of the need of our society. So, I'm not condoning violence or arrogance or impulsiveness. I'm saying that these are a part of the by-product of sitting on the lid for a very long time and failing to grasp the magnitude of the forces that were building up underneath.

Frick: You recognize not only the individual student needs but you see this in terms of the needs of the total society that have really been neglected here?

Murphy: Yes. I think the student can very well ask for the fulfillment of his own needs, but I don't think he can stop there. The student is a relatively fortunate person. The further he goes along with his education the more special and fortunate he is. There are a lot of people who don't have those privileges. The problem is really whether the educational system can reconstruct American life and world life fast enough to prevent the holocaust that otherwise I think is likely to come.

         ✿   ✿   ✿   ✿   ✿   ✿

Frick: Dr. Murphy, I would like to shift now to another theoretical question. You have supported what you have called a "soft determinism" approach in human development. You used that term in your book, *Human Potentialities.* [3] In talking about soft determinism you made the statement that "spontaneity in the sense of cause-lessness, we cannot use." Now, Abraham Maslow has done a lot of writing on unmotivated behavior or metamotivation, and I'm wondering if you reject this concept of Maslow's in the light of your statement on soft determinism?

Murphy: Well, I'm not familiar enough with Abe's writing to

---

[3] Gardner Murphy, *Human Potentialities* (New York: Basic Books, 1958).

handle it in the terms that you put to me. I'd rather simply say, as I
see the thing, the real philosophical issue is between "hard" deter
minism (as William James called it), and "soft" determinism. The
"hard" determinism is fatalism or external control over man. Man
is conceived to be the hapless pawn in the hands of vast cosmic
forces which he cannot control. "Soft" determinism says that man
is himself a *part* of the system of cosmic forces and these forces, so
to speak, flow through him. He represents a little sheltered struc
ture through which bio-chemical and physiological forces operate
and he does what is his nature to do. You find James, and many oth
ers of course, have developed this far more fully than I have in the
Human Potentialities book. I'm saying, essentially, that to protest
against being oneself is a rather empty kind of thing. The more
fully one develops into an understanding of one's situation, the
more likely one is to achieve some sort of freedom that means
something, which is an intelligent, thoughtful consideration of op
tions and selection of options which are realistic. But this is done by
virtue not of arbitrary spontaneity, as James would have said, but
by virtue of the utilization in a rational, orderly way, of the power
that one has as a living system. Now, that can be called determin
ism but it's not fatalism at all. It makes man a part of the causal se
quence.

Frick: It certainly involves choice, doesn't it? Man's ability or
power to choose is essential here.

Murphy: Yes, but the power to choose is itself the power to realize
what one is and therefore does not involve indeterminism. Most
people who talk about free will talk as if there were some freedom
in doing something alien to one's own nature and that, to me, is
senseless. I think to do something that is fully in accord with one
self, laid down by the nature of one's own being, can be called
"soft" determinism in James' sense of the term. I don't think there's
any escape hatch here, philosophically. I don't think that one can
then come back and say, when Oliver Cromwell decided to punish
the Irish for their role in the Civil War, "Too bad he did this, be
cause he could have done so many other things." I think this is non
sensical. I think Oliver Cromwell did what his military personality
and the kind of a person he was required, which was an essentially
sadistic thing.

Frick: Are you saying that he couldn't have acted in any other way, really?

Murphy: He had complete freedom in the sense that he had the freedom to be what he was. And that's exactly the kind of freedom that I hope for. I don't want to transcend myself by doing things alien to my nature.

✧   ✧   ✧   ✧   ✧   ✧

Frick: Dr. Murphy, in your book, *Encounter with Reality*,[4] you give a great deal of attention and support to the socialization of reality-seeking about which you say, "It is a matter of introducing levels of reality which are richer in value than those already existing in the individual." You have also suggested that by sharing in a group-defined world that we believe to be real, we let ourselves not only in for illusion, but for reality, not only for self-deception, but for social discovery. Now, Maslow has suggested as one major criterion of healthy personality, the transcendence of culture, or society. The ability, in other words, to say to hell with a value of society if the individual really is against this value system, and I'm wondering if you're in disagreement with this or not?

Murphy: No, I don't think there's any real difference of opinion. In my book, *Human Potentialities*, Part III: "Breaking Through The Mold" is concerned very much with the process which you quote from Maslow. It's the process by which one takes a critical and reconstructive attitude toward the cultural manifold that we're caught in. As a matter of fact, a lot of people have said this. You know the sociologist J. K. Folsom, almost forty years ago, set up the opposition between culture and creativity in a book that I read. I began to discover that anthropologists were very well aware of this fact; that culture can either be a flexible mold, or a tight, hard mold that's hard to cut through. So I'm glad the psychologists are waking up. I'm glad I had a chance to be one of those responding to this essentially anthropological discovery, I think.

Frick: This might be relevant to a previous question concerning self-consistency versus growth. I think that if we're bound by our

---

[4] Gardner Murphy and Herbert E. Spohn, *Encounter with Reality* (Boston: Houghton Mifflin Company, 1968).

culture, it does lead to certain rigidities in the individual personal
ity, wouldn't you say?

Murphy: Yes, but there are rigidities in the group situation which
are much more difficult to cope with than at the individual level
because we support each other and make a sort of fortress to resis
new possibilities. The individual, after all, is ultimately and as a
rule, at the mercy of the group rigidity. But there is very little, ac
tually, that the individual can ordinarily do to cut through the so
cial rigidities. The history of science has been largely a history of
the struggle of the investigator or his little group to cut through the
crystallized, dogmatic convictions prevalent in science as in other
fields in any given era. Quoting Abe, I think the best thing Abe ha
ever done, is *The Psychology of Science*.[5] It is a brilliant book in
which he has shown the crystallized nature of science and why only
a very human kind of approach can grasp the artificialities that are
involved in the scientific system.

✲   ✲   ✲   ✲   ✲   ✲

Frick: Dr. Murphy, in my interview with Dr. Maslow, he talked in
a rather humorous way about his "great fear and timidity," as he
called it, in presenting his unorthodox study on self-actualizing in
dividuals. He interpreted some of his dreams during this time as
being symbolic of his fears of being thrown out of the American
Psychological Association. You have also given a great deal of sup
port and encouragement to an unpopular area in psychology and
of course, I'm speaking of your interest in parapsychology and the
paranormal phenomena. You gave outspoken support to this area
when it was not popular and when it was not really acceptable or
respectable in psychology.

Murphy: It's not respectable at all. It's still anathema to over hal
the psychologists.

Frick: I'm wondering if you ever felt any anxiety over your profes
sional standing or personal development, for your support of these
phenomena?

Murphy: Sure, and I would want it to continue that way. It's going

---

[5] Abraham Maslow, *The Psychology of Science: A Reconnaissance* (New York: Harpe
and Row, 1966).

to take a very long time, much longer than my lifetime, to get these phenomena organized, documented, replicated, so that they are going to gradually find their way into the body of science. And in the meantime, they are so alien to the general organized forms of science that they are going to involve severe punishment—social and intellectual ostracism—directed against anybody. It's much harder on the young people who are trying to get themselves economically established. One of our major jobs is to encourage freedom and confidence among young psychologists, and people in other sciences, but it's not going to be an easy road for them. It never has been easy in the history of science for anything that's alien to the organized thought patterns.

Frick: Alien to the established laws that we work with . . .

Murphy: Yes, the understood ways, and of course it's largely 19th century physics that's making the trouble. It's not the middle of the 20th century physics. We seem to have more physicists studying and oriented toward serious consideration of extra-sensory perception, for example, than psychologists. This is because modern physics is a relatively flexible, intellectually rich and complex, rapidly flowing system of ideas. So you talk to a creative physicist and he begins to try to be helpful as to how his ideas might help you in *your* research. But you don't expect to find psychologists, for the most part, close enough to modern physics to understand. They're sure that in Newtonian terms, or even in 19th century terms, these phenomena are impossible, and that's all there is to it.

Frick: Well, Dr. Murphy, when you come out in your writings in support of parapsychology, and you have written some recent material on the paranormal phenomena, do you ever feel any real anxiety over your position in terms of your respectability among psychologists?

Murphy: Sure. You have to be realistic about that. Now a lot of people . . . there are two large classes of people. There are people who think that I'm irresponsible and misleading the youth like Socrates and worse, and then there are people who say I'm a nice guy and I'm generally respectable and everyone has his foibles, and what if Murphy has his own. . .

Frick: . . . he's only human, after all?

Murphy: Yes. You have to expect that. It's part of the game.

✿ ✿ ✿ ✿ ✿ ✿

Frick: Dr. Murphy, you've often addressed yourself to the union of human organisms with the material and social environment and the isomorphic relationship that can grow between them or that potentially exists between them. In pursuing this theme, you have said that man is a part of the sweep of the cosmos, and that he responds to cosmic patterns as an integral part of his self-structure. You are fond of saying, too, that "man resonates with cosmic structure as a part of his nature . . ." I have been greatly stimulated by these statements of yours that appear in your *Human Potentialities* book, but I have sometimes wished for specific examples of such resonance between man and the cosmos when I have been thinking about my own life. I wonder if you could give me some specific illustrations of this kind of union or isomorphic condition that can take place.

Murphy: Well, if you stand on the seashore and begin to analyze the different cadences, the different rising and falling sounds of the waves and the wind, you become aware of the fact that your own breathing, your own heartbeat, so far as you walk or run along the sand, the resonance of your own locomotion picks up the ultimate vibratory or other rhythmic patterns that are going on there. If you're interested in music you discover that the sound of the sigh or the exaltant shout, or the gentle up and down movements and cadences of the song of joy or a lullaby, are all incorporations of cosmic rhythms into the human rhythm. And it couldn't be anything else. If you go back to the evolutionary approach, to the beginning of respiratory function, traced down to the oxidative process; if you study the osmotic pressures, and the ways in which some substances are accumulated more and more within the living system until they reach a certain limit, and then begin to be excreted, or eliminated, you begin to realize that the life system has to be patterned on the rhythms of the world because it was constituted *out* of the rhythms of the world. And I think the same would be true of the cycles of the seasons. I've tried to do a study of Asian psychology. If you compare the psychology of India with the psychology of Greece, the differences are to a considerable extent explainable in terms of the fact that in the choppy, rapidly changing seasons with the alternate mountains and valleys as you travel through Greece, you get every mood being broken by a new mood. You have different aspects of nature different parts of the year in different parts of Greece. When you go to India you have the one great high plain, the Deccan Plain, which sweeps across all of India except the northern river valley. And this means that between the great Monsoons, a period of ten months, India presents you the same face continuously. You don't have rain, you don't have any unexpected heat or wind, for the most part. It's a stable . . . almost an eternity as you face it. And if you look at the actual texture of Greek psychology and Indian psychology, you would find that they arise, or appear to arise, to a considerable degree from these actual differences, as of course has been recognized by many historians and geographers. I would think you could pursue this right down to a good deal of detail. I think you could show that the ecology in terms of the physics, chemistry, geology, the meteorology and climatology to which man adapts, bring into his body the different rhythms, different patterns, in different parts of the world and at different times in history. So I don't think there's any mystery at all about man being isomorphic with the cosmic structure.

Frick: Would this include also, Dr, Murphy, an ability and sensitivity to perceive and react to cosmic patterns and to natural phenomena? Now I was thinking that not too long ago, following a gentle rain, there were drops of water on some bushes behind my house and every drop of water on every branch was serving as a prism as the sun began to shine through the bushes. I was quite taken by this scene because I could see hundreds and hundreds of miniature prisms. Would this be an example of resonating with the cosmic kind of materials that you're talking about—just the responding to this kind of thing here?

Murphy: Yes. You could take a particular kind of rhythm. Let's say, stating it carefully in mathematical terms, start with the spectrum, the solar spectrum or any other orderly presentation of light. Let's say the prism splitting like Newton—the white light into the component spectrum of colors—you can follow that through the water, you can follow it into the eye, and you can follow the relations the way Polyak did at the University of Chicago. Perhaps you can study this through to the visual purple and the action of the supporting cells, and retinal cells, the cones of the retina, you could go on through the optic chiasm to the occipital region of the brain and you could possibly show that the basic mathematical form has remained invariant. What's there in the sun, what's there in the water drop, what's there in the retina, what's there in the occipital lobe of the brain, are all one rhythm. It's not a series of billiard balls each one knocking the next one. It is probably the same wave form and, mathematically, the same expression all the way through. But, of course, this has been said by the neo-realists. E. B. Holt said this way back in 1912. It was said by Selig Hecht, the student of visual physiology and psychology. "Cast your material into invariant form," he used to say. You can get your phenomena to the point where you can see that you're not dealing with the whimsies of different media, but with the basic uniformity of the mathematical pattern.

Frick: But, Dr. Murphy, doesn't it depend, ultimately—when you say "cosmic consciousness"—this designates the importance, I think, of the *awareness* of one's world in response to one's own nature. I mean you can take this to any level and you can get very physiological and mathematical, but in terms of cosmic consciousness, this depends upon man's awareness of this kind of relationship with his environment, doesn't it?

Murphy: Well, I think for some people it does. But I think that the experiences called "cosmic consciousness" are widely variable. I think that the different disciplines which lead to so-called cosmic consciousness result in very different potentialities to be released in different people. I'm not convinced for example, that yoga and Zen Buddhism and psychedelic drugs and deep hypnosis produce identical states even though they may all be loosely called by some such name as cosmic consciousness. I think we don't know this field very well. I don't think that phenomenological descriptions are very good. I *do* think that cosmic consciousness in the sense of awareness of some sort of meaning of the universe as a whole, is accessible to widely varying kinds of people depending partly on the culture but very largely on other variables we don't know about. There's a beautiful study in the journal *Daedalus* in 1959 by Edith Cobb,[6] de-

---

[6] Edith Cobb, "Daedalus," Journal of the American Academy of Arts and Sciences (Summer 1959).

scribing the experiences of this kind of universal awareness in small children. She has collected hundreds and hundreds of childrens' reports on this early sense. It is very similar to what you get in Wordsworth's *Ode on Intimations of Immortality*. It is the experience of the small child in belonging, not just to his parents, or not just to his home, but somehow to this whole universe. What this ultimately means, I don't think I know, but I would include it among the universally accessible testimony to experiencing something that transcends the competitive individual.

Frick: . . . right, the competitive striving . . . There's a great deal in your use of the concept of cosmic consciousness and the idea that man is a part of the sweep of the cosmos. I think there's a lot of similarity between this concept and Maslow's "peak" experience, or maybe going back even to Freud's "oceanic feeling." And, of course, it's also called the "mystical experience," in more religious terms.

Murphy: Yes, but I think that these terms are very hard to define. The term "mystical" is one with exceptionally broad connotations. Abe's "peak experiences" we don't really know about. I had a talk with Abe about this a dozen years ago and he told me reasons which I accepted as to why they could not be fully verbalized and why he could not share them. This has always been the testimony of mystics. They can say a few things and then they crumple up in the sense of the inadequacy of words to describe this, and this makes the comparability of Zen Buddist satori, and the Hinduism Samadhi and the Western World sense of the loss of individuality, and the Nirvana experience difficult. All these things probably overlap some but I don't think we have a good descriptive and explanatory psychology of these experiences. I would be very reluctant to say they're identical. I would be very reluctant to say that Abe's peak experiences are identical with Wordsworth's experiences in *Tintern Abbey* which they can be compared with. I think they have some halo, some emotional overtone which can be shared, but not substance for substance equated, I wouldn't think.

Frick: I'm wondering . . . you seem to feel in your book *Human Potentialities*, and also in your more recent book *Encounter with Reality*, that it's very much a part of . . . or among man's most precious human potentials to be able to resonate with cosmic structure and

cosmic materials and to be able to experience this kind of identification. I'm wondering how we can educate young people to have
this kind of concept and projection of their own growth and development. This seems to be something that should concern education
and I'm not sure we're really concerned or doing anything about it.

Murphy: Well, there are a great many routes to this goal. I'm not
convinced that we have any way of evaluating which are the best
routes for different people. When I saw my wife teaching Sara
Lawrence girls eighteen and twenty years old the appreciation of
small children, helping them to understand and to love small children, I would say that hardly anything in human life could be more
beautiful or more magnificent. Then I see Abe Maslow having a
peak experience; I see Mike Murphy out at Esalen encouraging
people in various types of out-reaching experiences, even excite-
ment about the ability to touch another human being; I read the accounts of psychedelic experiences of many sorts; and hear the
words of travelers about the uniqueness of certain experiences, let's
say in a Zen training program; I don't feel that we know what's the
best. In fact, I'm not sure we even have any criteria for saying
what's the best. Even when I'm very close to these things as I was
to my wife's experience with Sara Lawrence girls and the nursery
school children with whom they worked, I don't pretend to understand this. I don't know to what extent psychoanalytic concepts of
identification or Erik Erikson's ideas of identity, or some of the
modern ideas about the loss of ego boundaries—the depersonaliza-
tion or removal of all individuality in experience—I don't know
how far these are useful ideas. And I get a little restless when somebody comes back from India or from Esalen and says "We've got
the answer." I don't believe there's any one answer. I think there
are many routes, many interesting things along the way but we do
have an obligation to students to warn them against cul-de-sacs,
and against dangerous pits. We get off of our known route into the
unknown and see all sorts of odd effects. I would feel that the problem is a research problem today and not a problem of evangelism. I
think that we have suddenly dumped our student world into a
whole, rich, complicated sink of unknown or not well understood
human experiences and more or less said "sink or swim." And I just
don't think we have that right, if one speaks morally, except under

very carefully safeguarded conditions where careful observations can be made. I do think we have to go on studying LSD–25 and mescaline and the rest of them on a scientific basis, the way they are doing in a few medical centers. But I think just saying that the student has a right to new experiences ignores the vast, dark uncertainties and the same is true for not only drugs, but the same is true of almost any radical method of self-examination if it involves getting off by oneself in a special brotherhood or a sisterhood in which each encourages the other to get some unusual type of experience, and they're not subject to any social discipline or any careful concern for the consequences of such extreme isolation and burying oneself in a new criterion of life. I think these things involve very considerable hazards.

Frick: Without being impertinent, Dr. Murphy, I think that some of your writings have done as much as any other writings in recent years, to take us into the unknown, and to give a certain amount of respectability to it. Do you feel any qualms about any of your writings in this area at all? As you speak of responsibility here, I think . . .

Murphy: Well, I don't ever know whether the evaluative statements and the precautionary statements are properly phrased or directed to the right people. I do believe, for example, in the very great importance of research on psychedelic drugs as I just said, and I believe at the same time they involve great risks. Well, in Sidney Cohen's book [7] on psychedelic drugs for which I wrote the introduction, there is the appeal for the recognition of very new information, and at the same time the recognition of the hazards which are involved except in the most careful medical supervision. I may have been unwise in the phrasing, I don't know. I may have been incompletely forthright in regard to the uncertainties of all that West Coast psychedelic research about which I know something. There are several different places in California in which there has been a good deal of bold experimentation and I may have been inadequately sensitive to some of the problems. I still don't know that. Certainly, as far as psychical research is concerned I

---

[7] Sidney Cohen, *The Beyond Within: The LSD Story* (New York: Antheneum, 1964).

pointed out the enormous importance of understanding these strange experiences more adequately and at the same time may have been insufficiently clear that for some people the cultivation of the world of the paranormal may at times be unsound. It depends on the person, the supervision, and the moral strength of the group, I mean their loyalty to each other. It's just got to be said over again: there *are* risks involved in extending the horizons. If you push to gain more information about human nature or about social life, you're going to keep on encountering unknowns that are somewhat threatening to some people. I think you have to take those risks. If I said an insufficient amount about the fact of the risks, let me say again I think that any attempt to push the horizons far, give a person new areas of experience, involves problems. Depending upon the strength of the person and the strength of the people working with him there may have to be different kinds of restraints, different kinds of disciplines used. It's a personal matter with individual hazards which often simply have to be faced.

✿   ✿   ✿   ✿   ✿   ✿

Frick: Dr. Murphy, I would like to get less theoretical now, and a little more personal for a few minutes if you don't mind. We've been talking a great deal about parapsychology and extra sensory perception, cosmic consciousness and so forth. I'm interested in how you became interested in such phenomena. I feel certain that it wasn't a part of your formal training in psychology. I wonder if you could comment on this, and then I would like to ask you for a couple of personal experiences if there are any.

Murphy: Well, I've told the story several times about my reading in my grandfather's library at 16 years of age William Barrett's book, *Psychical Research.*[8] I read that book with great delight and made up my mind it was very important. It was one of the factors that led me to major in psychology at Yale, and at that time, the junior and senior years, I made up my mind that I was going to go into psychical research. That was somewhat dominant over my second choice which would have been to be a neurologist, or a neurologist and psychiatrist. I decided that I did not need the medical

---

[8] William Barrett, *Psychical Research* (New York: Henry Holt, 1911).

training and that I did need a Ph.D. in psychology, and I went on to Harvard and then to Columbia, insistently spending a great deal of my time studying the best material in psychical research. In my first graduate year at Columbia I gave two hours a day, systematically, to reading psychical research. I read the massive literature of the London Society for Psychical Research, and then I decided I hadn't been doing it real justice and so the second year I was there I gave three hours a day right straight through. I led a completely double life because, of course, the other graduate students had no respect or interest in it, nor did the staff have any respect nor interest in it, but I believed that it was right and I continued. When I got a chance I did some research in the field and over the last 50 years I have put in a very considerable part of my professional life into reading, discussing, supervising, and working with research people in this field. Now, I am not, personally, a so-called sensitive subject. I am not a big-time ESP subject. I've had interesting experiences as everybody has had which can be called coincidences or whatever you like but nothing that would be important enough to write home about in their own right. However, I don't base my faith in these realities upon so-called personal experiences but upon scientific study of published evidence and the witnessing of experiments and participation in the research group activities.

Frick: Have you had any outstanding . . . I go back to this term cosmic consciousness which you've used a number of times. I wonder if you've had any experiences of cosmic consciousness that might in some way be similar to what Maslow terms "peak experience?"

Murphy: No. No. There's no use equivocating about that. The answer is a flat "no." I have not had Maslow's type. I know what he's talking about, because I've read dozens and dozens of careful descriptions, but I've not had them myself.

        ✧   ✧   ✧   ✧   ✧   ✧

Frick: Dr. Murphy, your major work in personality theory, *Personality: A Biosocial Theory,* was an extremely eclectic work and has been called this by reviewers and writers, and I would like to know if you've moved away from an eclectic position in recent years. It seems to me that you have been moving somewhat more towards a self-realization theory, and . . .

Murphy: No, I have very scant respect for this word "eclectic." In the introduction to the Basic Books edition of this re-published study just a few years ago, I said that such a book as this is likely to be called "eclectic." The word means two very different things: (1) the juxtaposition of fragments from different systems effecting a loose federation of essentially unrelated ideas; (2) the organization of a coherent theoretical system into which observations from different viewpoints can be integrated. It is in the second sense that I respect and try to accept this conception. And I remain in that same position today.

Frick: Would you say that since you have written this book which has been a number of years ago, you've moved more toward a self-realization theory of personality?

Murphy: No, I'm very uncomfortable with these phrases. I attended a meeting of the Humanistic Psychology group and some of their leaders in Connecticut. You perhaps know about that meeting about four years ago. And I was delighted to see that almost every person in the group said that there is much too much vague uplift talk going on and too little concrete discussion of how self-actualization can be achieved, how it can be recognized, investigated, measured, and so forth. You would have to have a positive program. I am restless, really. Year after year we go on with both the leaders and followers talking about undefined concepts and the idea of self-realization strikes me as really incapable of being defined along these lines. I tried to indicate at the beginning when I was talking about Goldstein versus the Gestaltists that we're moving towards an undefined ideal, I think. I have a further difficulty. It seems to me that every individual represents many potential selves, and to say "self-actualization" implies that there's just *one* potential self, and that the business of the human individual is to achieve it or complete it or express it. I don't believe that. I believe that the stuff of human nature in its general and in its individual form is very rich in open potentialities for movement in many possible directions, and I think we blind ourselves to this openness when we talk as if there were one route that the individual must follow towards self-actualization. I think many people reading Maslow or Rogers or Gordon Allport or any of the other leaders, have come through with an essentially polished, finished kind of personality, which is not at all what the authors would have intended. Gordon Allport would never have meant to be understood that way and yet I think that the concept of self-actualization lends itself to that interpretation. I hope the time will come when we talk about the realization of potentials or of multiple selves or something of this sort. We're desperately afraid of such. We think we're talking about Dr. Jekyll and Mr. Hyde. We must recognize the fact that each child has many potential selves depending upon what the environment has to offer and particularly what parents, school, and siblings offer by way of reciprocity, by something to interact with.

Frick: Yes. But isn't this where we meet the importance of choice and the freedom of choice that the individual has for determining what directions he wishes to take and what potentials he is really committed to?

Murphy: Yes, if one makes a reasonably systematic use of the idea of openness and flexibility, mobilizing all that one has in the making of the choice rather than being limited to one traditional direction in which one must move. One has to face the fact that in the world of today there are bewildering possibilities all of the time. Just take the vocational sphere alone. We only go back a few generations until the father largely dominated the son's vocational choice. Now we have a dictionary of occupations, we have organized information of many types showing what kind of preparation we need for what kind of roles of activity. The trouble is, you still don't really tell the story like it is, because it's even more complex. I was just talking to a very able dentist about how he was given the Kuder and the Strong interest tests and intelligence tests and so forth, and was told at the end of his sophomore year, I think it was, that he would be a good dentist. Well, they didn't study his interpersonal relations. They didn't study the way in which he cared for the patient and the patient's wife and children as they waited in the office. They didn't consider the hazards that the man would find with people who use their teeth, so to speak, as a screen for a psychiatric difficulty. Thousands of difficulties we can think of that are not candidly spelled out and can't be candidly spelled out to a sophomore that wants vocational guidance. The real fact is that just practicing dentistry in Washington, D. C., which sounds like a very simple thing, can really lead into many different ways of looking at human beings and helping them or injuring them. Well, I think this particular man that I'm talking about was given very effective guidance, but many others that I have seen in the United States and some other places, in medical, dental and other remedial services, have not been given an idea of the real complexity. I see clinical psychology students still that don't seem to have read what was found out at Ann Arbor about the enormous number of mistakes that are made in guiding people into clinical psychology or in trying to practice clinical psychology, because they've oversimplified the job. So when somebody says he's a "born clinician," I just shudder.

✿   ✿   ✿   ✿   ✿   ✿

Frick: Dr. Murphy, you have said that there is a katydid nature to scrape, a frog nature to croak, and a warbler nature to warble and that it's human nature to play *Air for G String* on a stradivarius. You have also concerned yourself with the things a species tends to learn, and interests and directions taken when the species is free to choose. Rogers, in a similar vein, says that people in psychotherapy, if really free to choose, go in certain directions. And I wonder if your statements suggest your support or faith in a naturalistic value system. I think you hint at this at times, but I'm really not sure how you feel about this.

Murphy: Yes, I firmly believe in a naturalistic value system. I believe that wants and sympathy and the enjoyment of fellow feeling, resonance of one person to another, are just as biological as eating. I think that these root component factors in a human ethical system are very genuine, and can be built on. I think the aggressions are likewise very genuine and real. I think that the environmental conditions—physical and social conditions—will play a very large part in releasing one or another system of natural biological tendencies. Now, on the other issue, man being a kind of an organism that does things that are not biologically predictable at such a simple level, I think the point is that anthropology and paleontology have given us a lot of evidence recently of the amazing rate at which man developed relatively undifferentiated or unspecialized brain tissue. Go back a million years if you like, it is only a moment in geological time, and you find that man is developing a vast associative network of potential learning, perceiving, thinking activities, and that these very rich possibilities act to make his sights, his hearings, his smellings, his touchings, much more complex, more interesting, and capable of aesthetic development. Art forms begin to emerge as he shapes a stone into something he needs to use to scrape or strike with. It has its own intrinsic, delighful quality. That aesthetic factor begins to appear in the same way that preliterate societies developed all sorts of musical instruments to enjoy the tones, the rhythms, the cadences, the multi-instrument orchestration and so forth which make up the aesthetic delights of music. Now if you say that these things serve a biological purpose, I will agree with you. However, they don't serve a *survival* purpose in any obvious sense, but rather they add to the enrichment of experience. When I'm talking about man playing the *Air for G String* on a stradivarius, it is that he takes the primitive auditory satisfactions of the pure tone and he elaborates this in all sorts of ways and that is a biological funtion but it is also a cultural function. It's a bridge—over from a biological to a cultural function, so that I think I would agree fully with Rogers and Maslow and others who talk about hierarchies of needs, but I would *not* be inclined to say that any of these more complex needs are secondary to, or subserviant to others. In fact, we all know musicians who are very reluctant to go and get a bowl of soup if they can hear another Toscanini record or whatever it is. It has its own intrinsic "functional autonomy," Allport would have said, or some "canalized" value I would have said. There are other ways of phrasing this capacity to make something very rich out of something potentially also very simple.

Frick: Dr. Murphy, you do accept, then, a kind of a naturalistic or biological base for human values and I would like to know, also, if you feel that there are universal criteria for healthy personality?

Murphy: Yes, but on an empirical basis I don't think we know an awful lot. I think we can state some of these things negatively by speaking of the conflicts, the humiliations, and the guilts that contribute to the suffering of children and prevent their growing into effective or happy adulthood. In fact, I think we can lay down on the basis of modern psychiatric experience quite a lot of simple rules of thumb regarding how to prevent these things, particularly the humiliation, shame and guilt which do such a great deal of damage to the normal development of a healthy ego and sense of adequacy, a sense of worth. But I don't think that these negative rules are anywhere near enough. I think that the discovery of enrichment of one's own individuality through commerce with others, through conversations, through play, through love, through social intergrative activity, is still largely carried out at an intuitive level. I've just been hearing this noon, before I came over here, about a couple of young clinicians who, as they were described, were over-involved. That is to say they got so deeply concerned with the problems of the patient that they had no perspective. I presume they meant for other people who were on their list of patients or to the families of these particular patients, or to their own future needs to learn and to report adequately on experience. This over-involvement would be pretty good proof that the individual doesn't know how to control, how to discipline, how to draw firm barriers on his impulsive out-going response. You read about Jesus going into the desert or up into the high mountains when the multitudes got too thick, needing some time by himself, and Schweitzer, and other modern Messianic figures will remind you that the best we have, still, is an intuitive response: "How much can I give? Well, I'll give a lot until I'm drained, and then maybe I'll have to stop giving." We don't really have an orderly disciplined scheme of how to cultivate, with impunity, warm and rich social relationships. We know we need them but we don't know how to tell a wife or a daughter or a friend, "You're giving too much, you've got to stop," although we see the need. In other words, we have good rule of thumb principles, and they can be delved into with the most elaborate type of ethics. I know people who seem to think that Dr. Schweitzer, for example, achieved a complete ideal of modern rule of life, and I feel equally clear that having seen some Gandhis and some Nehrus, and some Schweitzers in action, it is pretty clear that we don't have a specific applicable modern ethics except in the most rudimentary form. And I say again that the negative influences we can tell pretty clearly, that this treatment or influence would involve damage to your patient or to your child. But what's too much? What are the ground rules for an effective use of, say, a clinician's or a social worker's time? I listen to them and I get the impression that they're not too sure themselves. We need the spadework for developing an orderly disciplined conception which would not be restraining and inhibiting, but that job remains to be done.

Frick: Dr. Murphy, you've written a great deal about the human potential, and you've expressed concerns about its development, its enhancement and fulfillment and, yet, I've never read any explicitly stated theory of healthy personality in any of your writings. I've tried to develop one but I would like for you to characterize healthy personality if you could, and this is perhaps an unfair question right now, because it's a very, very difficult and complex kind of issue, but I wonder if you could comment on this.

Murphy: . . . well, from my limited angle, that's the same question that I just answered. In a purely negative way, I think you can say that there are certain things that inhibit the development of a normal personality, particularly guilt, shame, the bitterness of self-blame, etc. I don't have anything to add to that. On the positive side, I think we can say in a bland, general way, love, generosity, support, a reasonable amount of balance, poise, self-control, all these things are in the right direction. But how to make a mish-mash, how to make a goulash, a hash out of all these ingredients? The super cook that has the ability to tell us how to make a really magnificent French dish out of these things . . . we still rely on the journalist and the novelist to tell us this. I don't believe the psychologist knows any more about healthy personality than a playwright or a novelist. I don't think it has reached a scientific level yet.

Frick: Do you think we will reach that level in psychology?

Murphy: Yes, by gradually being more specific in the use of terms, by being more exact, by giving examples, and by noticing exaggerations. Of course, the further discovery of the biology of human nature as we learn about it through sensory deprivation studies, sensory enrichment studies, and as we learn the powers of self-understanding, self-control that comes with these modern techniques of sensory enrichment, internal scanning, etc., we may know enough about our internal world, we may interpret the messages from the viscera and the muscles more and more accurately, so as to understand the basis for a rhythm and order in living; understand the marginal messages from the vital organs that relate to our aesthetic experience like the rhythms that I mentioned, or the responses to cosmic order. All of this will come. I have a piece, incidentally, in the *American Psychologist* which has just been accepted, and will appear in a few months. It is called, "Psychology in the Year 2000," [9] which was derived from that talk that I mentioned that I gave for Ross Stagner at Wayne State University. In this article I tried to develop this "internal scanning" theme. I believe the psychology of the next 30 years is going to be very rich in self-discovery of the scientific sort. And, of course, it will share with the self-discovery of the humanistic and religious and mystical and other types. So I think that your question can be answered when we have a lot more data. I just don't think right now that I could tell a twenty year old anything much that he or she didn't know about achieving a healthy personality. I say try to understand yourself and try to understand the people around you and have hope that more generous and less self-accusing attitudes will develop.

Frick: Dr. Murphy, would . . . I keep referring to the term "cosmic consciousness" because I think you employ it as an important concept in some of your later writings. I'm wondering if you give any important place in healthy personality to man's ability to sense and relate and resonate with cosmic structure.

Murphy: Well, I'm sympathetic to what I hear about these people but I don't really have enough first-hand experience to say that. If you gave me information regarding each of the next ten people that come into this office as to what kind of cosmic orientation they had and you asked me to predict how well adjusted they were in their everyday lives, I wouldn't expect the two to be correlated. I wouldn't expect that I would know how to use one to predict the other. In fact it may be a highly individualized matter. It may be that somebody might follow Abe Maslow's scheme and come out on the opposite end of the opera glass and *not* develop the characteristics that Abe says have come with his orientation. Abe is highly individualized and so are most of these people. I'm quite sure that if I attempted to be a mystic I'd be a terrible mess and I can enormously respect people who are mystics without being one myself.

✿ ✿ ✿ ✿ ✿ ✿

Frick: Dr. Murphy, what are your chief professional involvements

[9] Gardner Murphy, "Psychology in the Year 2000," *American Psychologist*, 24 (May, 1969). Presented to the Wayne State University Centennial Symposium, Detroit, Michigan, May 10, 1968

and interests at the present time? And I wonder if you would tell me something of your plans for the future.

Murphy: Yes, well, I have a light load here at George Washington. Technically, I am on a full time basis but that's a very generous appellation. I'm teaching two seminars and I have four students working on individual reading with me and one Ph.D. student. I go up to New York at present, every two weeks for a day. I teach a class in History and Systems at City College on alternate Wednesdays. When I'm in New York I give all the rest of that day to the American Society for Psychical Research, of which I'm President now. I carry on a very large correspondence with experimental people in psychical research, notably, with Dr. Ullman at Maimonides Hospital in Brooklyn, with Gertrude Schmeidler at City College, with Thelma Moss at UCLA, and I do have a fairly heavy administrative responsibility to keep things moving on what I consider a constructive direction at the American Society. I'm also involved in a great deal of correspondence accumulated over the years. For example, as a result of going to India twenty years ago, I have about a hundred regular Indian correspondents and it's quite a considerable bulk of mail. It is the same for Columbia days, for City College days. Everything I've done in my life has led into ongoing communications. The Menninger Foundation has been generous enough to give me a full-time secretary although I'm only out there a few days a month. She is a very excellent secretary who has worked with me and being a very competent, devoted person, she enables me to carry this huge volume of correspondence so that people are puzzled when they get letters that have obviously been written and typed in Topeka, Kansas. I have been out there with the Menninger Foundation for the last fifteen years. I'm also trying to read. As a companion volume to the *Asian Psychology* that my wife and I edited last summer I have a volume in press called *Western Psychology*, from the Greeks to the end of the 19th century with William James, and there will be other companion volumes in that series. I'm planning a book on *Overcoming Self-Deception*, which is a follow-up on my book *Encounter with Reality*. There are also small research and writing jobs which I can't start on now until the others are out of the way. But we have our summers . . . we have a full ten weeks in our place in New Hampshire which makes

big progress possible in the matter of writing. I carry a dictaphone
up there and the book on *Overcoming Self-Deception* will be done
there. I'm about two-thirds through a revision of the *Historical Introduction* which will be published, maybe a year and a half from
now, and I have a systematic book on *Psychical Research*, which I
have over half written which I hope will also be done there if I live
and if my health remains fairly good, which it is at present. Next
summer will see those two last books, *Historical Introduction* and
Psychical Research pretty far along. So you see it's a rather scattered life and if you ask me where I want to focus, I would say,
"I'm like a man taking hold of several live wires at once. I don't
know how to let go." I would certainly not give up psychical research. It's enormously important to me and several big breakthroughs are appearing right now. What Ullman is doing at Maimonides Medical Center in Brooklyn, what Karlis Osis is doing at the
American Society itself, what Gertrude Schmeidler is doing at City
College, what Thelma Moss is doing at UCLA, are all very important breakthroughs. And I'm not going to abandon the field. I also
don't want to get outside the academic world. There are all together too many precious associations that would be lost if I had no
academic connections. And I have a good faculty here to associate
with and I'm in sympathy with the kind of work that is being done
around me, and I enjoy the students, so I have no plans for immediate retirement. My wife, of course, being seven years younger than
I and in good health, will continue in her research with children
and that's one of the major factors in making me unwilling to make
any big change. She has a position here at the Children's Hospital.
And if that work continues and is properly funded by federal support we won't change our basic plan of life for the present.

Frick: Dr. Murphy, what's the nature of the work you're doing for
the Menninger Foundation? I believe you told me you just spend
two or three days a month out there.

Murphy: . . . writing and consulting, mainly. Actually I go out there
Thursday afternoons once a month and stay until Monday after-
noon, a long weekend. It will be somewhat more next year, probably. I expect to be there five or six days each month if I can work it
out. I consult with four or five of the project directors. You see, I've
been there . . . I served as Director of Research for 15 years.

Frick: Is this still your title, or is this changed now?

Murphy: No, Professor of Psychology at George Washington University is my current title. They probably will give me some sort of honorific title. I was Henry March Pfeiffer Professor out at Menninger's and I think they're going to call me Pfeiffer Professor Emeritus, so I'm told. [10] And that will mean a little more than a nominal connection. It will mean a working connection with all the projects' directors. You see, these projects grew up during the period that I was Director of Research and I'm quite close to the men who are leading these studies so I shall continue to work with them as a consultant. And then, of course, all this writing that I was describing to you, as I said, is made possible by my secretary who is a Menninger secretary and it's possible for them . . .

Frick: . . . so she handles all this for you?

Murphy: Certainly. I couldn't do any of this without her.

Frick: Dr. Murphy, you mentioned some key breakthroughs in psychical research and I wonder if you could just mention one of these, perhaps, for the record.

Murphy: Well, what Montague Ullman and his associates have been doing at Maimonides Hospital in Brooklyn is a modern utilization of the sleep-dreams laboratory of the Kleitman-Dement type, where it is possible under proper safeguards to have the content of a pictorial presentation transmitted telepathically from a distant sender to a sleeping subject. The technique has to be very elaborate as far as controls are concerned but it is not elaborate from a conceptual point of view. It's a very simple thing: Can you demonstrate significantly and with replication over and over again, that at a considerable distance, 110 feet, with four closed doors between, randomly selected visual material—paintings—can be transmitted to show up in the content of the dreaming of a distant individual? And they've been at this several years now and have published quite a good deal. I think the results are quite clear-cut.

Frick: That's really exciting.

Murphy: Yes, I think it is quite clear-cut. Oh, it will go through a

---

[10] Dr. Murphy was made Pfeiffer Professor Emeritus, February, 1969.

long period of challenge and replication and challenge and replication, but there has been some replication both there and elsewhere. There are several other studies but that would be the one I would emphasize most at this time.

Frick: You know, the sad part about it, I think, is that so very few psychologists are really in a frame of mind or spirit to be open to these findings.

Murphy: Sure, but what are you going to do?

Frick: Plug away, I guess.

Murphy: You catch them when they're young and they're eager and they're capable of developing a discipline appropriate to the investigation. We have a good deal of success there. We've had, oh, young folks like Charley Tart at the University of California at Davis who has been at it in recent years. He is a very competent, able guy with an open mind and a high experimental productivity. It only takes two or three in a generation, if they're really first-class, to open up a field.

✧　　✧　　✧　　✧　　✧　　✧

Frick: Dr. Murphy, in my talk with Dr. Maslow a couple of months ago, he indicated that he was devoting most of his life now to his theoretical interests and he was rather sad as he talked about giving up many of the things he enjoyed to pursue more vigorously his theories and his writings. For example, he said he has stopped going to plays and stopped going on nature walks and other things like this that he really enjoyed very much. I'm wondering if your development is tending to go in the same direction as you move toward the end of your professional career. Could you comment on this for me?

Murphy: Well, of course one fights a rear-guard action against old age but I do walk quite a lot and my wife greatly enjoys walking, particularly in the warmer part of the year. We have our place in New Hampshire and we make the most of it. We're outdoors a great deal and we hike and canoe and we enjoy the outside world. Our grandchildren visit us up there and so forth. During the dead of winter it's difficult to get out enough and there is a danger of losing tonus, but since my eyes and ears are all right and I can do the usual academic stuff, I don't think I'm losing ground very fast. If I can go on this way, I will just gracefully taper off a little bit. I don't expect to retire, I expect only to taper off as I may have to.

Frick: Are you keeping up an interest in hobbies and other things non-professional right along?

Murphy: Well, the same things . . . music means a great deal to my wife and me. We have a son and his wife in New York who are very musical. We have a daughter and her husband and four grandchildren whom we see very frequently and they keep us oriented to many young interests. I don't think there has been any great change in recent years. I read a good deal. I have a lot of visits, so I don't . . . I wouldn't say that I feel any serious restrictions at present.

       ✿   ✿   ✿   ✿   ✿   ✿

Frick: Dr. Murphy, you've been a part of American psychology and a very important part of its growth and development over the last few decades. What major directions do you see American psychology taking in the next decade. Do you discern any major trends here?

Murphy: Well, more and more towards extreme sophistication in method. I think it's methodologically a very devoted and very intense kind of a world that we live in and psychology has rapidly given up the diverse, confused, many-sided shape that it had. You and I are both fighting a rather unsuccessful rear-guard action against specialization and quantification. Abe Maslow can get to be elected by a miracle to be President of the APA and one has to study a lot of politics to understand that but all the big plums, everywhere at all the levels, are tending more and more to go to the brilliantly sophisticated, experimental design, statistics, mathematical models, ultra-scientific scientist. And that's one of the things that Abe takes apart in his book on the *Psychology of Science.* I think that's going to continue. I think the prestige is there and the satisfaction of getting replicable results. Psychology can be squeezed into a mechanical form the way other sciences have been, and there's less to resist. After all, physics has got enough open space to move around in so that contrary alien theories can be thrown up a dime a dozen every year and physicists, as long as they're brilliant and creative and mathematical, can't be laughed at for dreaming up a new theory, but the less mature sciences can't afford that luxury. They're going to have to be scientific in the scientist sense of the term and there's no other direction to go. And so the rest of us who happen to be more diffuse or variegated or flexible, or whatever you want to call it are going to have to be content to be voices crying in the wilderness for awhile.

Frick: You've played this role for a long time, haven't you, Dr. Murphy?

Murphy: Well, yes, it's a very great satisfaction to see every now and again, one of one's pupils like Muzafer Sherif or Ted Newcomb or Ren Likert who get very much in a central position when doing something that's not a part of the orthodox, official movement. I was quite amused, by the way, to see what happened when Muzafer Sherif got one of the three APA research prizes this year. Muzafer came to me at Columbia in 1935–36, and we worked together. He was all full of ideas as to how the ultra-objectivism of Floyd Allport could be replaced by a direct perceptual study of participation in a social group, a study of the experience of the individual himself. And he did that study magnificently, as you know. Now, in 1968, he gets the prize and the little spiel that is written in honor of Muzafer talks about how tough and hard-boiled, how objective and scientific he was in the work that he did . . . because that's the Zeitgiest. Now, one has to have a sense of humor.

✿   ✿   ✿   ✿   ✿   ✿

Frick: Dr. Murphy, how do you feel about the humanistic . . . the so-called third-force movement in psychology today?

Murphy: Well, it worries me, it frightens me, it gives me . . . as the old spiritual says, "it causes me to tremble." I don't know where it's going. I got a letter from Dr. Sutich some time ago indicating that they got a thousand subscriptions, I believe, a thousand subscribing readers of the *Journal of Humanistic Psychology* and now they're ready for another kind of effort which is beyond psychology and beyond personality, apparently.

Frick: Yes, what's the name of that new journal?[11]

Murphy: Isn't it *Transpersonal*?

---

[11] *The Journal of Transpersonal Psychology.*

Frick: Yes, I believe that's it.

Murphy: Well, I don't think we've digested our breakfast and we are ordering a big lunch. I'm having a hard time seeing what's really new and sound in the humanistic psychology and I think it will take quite a while. I don't see why all of these articles have to appear in a new journal. I was told, and it may well be true, that it was because the APA editors wouldn't publish any such stuff. Maybe this is the reason but I don't think it's the only reason, because I think a lot of people including Abe, including Gordon Allport and Carl Rogers, have a very big public following. I never felt any ungenerous response to my stuff even though it is off the beaten track.

Frick: Maybe they're able to accomplish this by the sheer force of their reputations whereas many lesser knowns would have a real struggle here.

Murphy: Well, all right, I have no quarrel with it. Is the message of humanistic psychology a solid, sound, thoughtful, orderly presentation of very important issues? Well, okay, if it is, more power to it. The few articles that have actually come through to me have not had very much to offer and I haven't felt that they needed a journal. I told you about one humanistic meeting I went to. I went to another. I went to the APA Humanistic Psychology group meeting in Washington, in the fall of 1967.

Frick: You were on a panel at that meeting, weren't you?

Murphy: Yes. I just don't feel that they have a very great deal that's new to offer but I may very well be wrong and I'd be willing to suspend judgment for a few years. I just say "Let's use the same careful standards that we would use in any other kind of scientific effort." If they would say, "We're not trying to be scientists," I would say, "Okay, then you've got the whole world of literature and philosophy and if this is your message, fine. But if by humanistic psychology you mean you're going to do more than the playwright and the novelist and the historian can do; if you're going to attempt the discipline of a psychology, a scientific study, then meet the standards of science."

Frick: Then you feel they're not really doing this right now.

Murphy: Well, I haven't seen the stuff. I . . . the whole business of a third force in psychology implies that it's within psychology. It implies that along with behaviorism and psychoanalysis, another scientific effort must be made. I don't feel that hostile to psychoanalysis. I've probably learned more from Freud than from any other one person. I think behaviorism is pretty shallow but I still have learned a lot, particularly from Pavlov, who was very hard-boiled and anti-psychological, but I still learned a lot from him. I don't see the need for crying on the housetops the importance of science unless the methods of science and the canons and the criteria of excellence which obtain in scientific work, are going to be applied to some degree.

✿   ✿   ✿   ✿   ✿   ✿

Frick: Dr. Murphy, you have called for new and creative ways of utilizing group organization and group life. I'm wondering if you see the recent flourishing of T-groups and sensitivity training groups, as a viable effort in this direction?

Murphy: Well, I can only say so being outside the ballpark you know, or seeing a fly come over the fence once in a while. I'm not there on the inside. I have never gone to Bethel or any of the other training centers. I hear a lot of talk and I think it is interesting. And if there is a lot of verbiage, a lot of cultist jargon, well, that's true of most new movements. No, I don't really think I have much to offer on that.

Frick: Thank you very much, Dr. Murphy.

3

Interview with
Dr. Carl Rogers

La Jolla, California January 24, 1969

'rick: Dr. Rogers, I think my first introduction to you was in 1951 when I read your book on client-centered psychotherapy. I've been eading your material ever since. I must say, before I start these questions, that you've been very influential in my own development both personally and professionally. However, I think this morning I would like to play the devil's advocate and ask some questions in reas that trouble me a bit as well as other types of questions later on.

One of the things that troubles me sometimes, regarding self-actualizing theory, is its deterministic treatment of human development. That is, it seems that many self-actualizing theorists place great deal of emphasis on an organic or biological base to human trivings. Maslow has his instinctoid needs and you have your own way of saying this. The self-actualizing theorists talk about discovering the self and the existentialists talk about creating the self and here's a very different emphasis here. I think this is highlighted in 'ictor Frankl's article, *Beyond Self-Actualization and Self-Expression,* where he criticizes self-actualization theory and says that "we ave neglected that sphere of human existence in which man hooses what he will do and what he will be." [1] Now, do you feel hat the self-actualizing theories and your own "self theory" are in basic conflict with the existentialists over freedom of choice?

ogers: No, I really don't. Let's see if I can get in a theoretical hood this morning. I think that you're right that I do see a biological base to human development. That, to me, doesn't seem strange. think you see it in plant life, animal life, that the individual organ-

---

[1] Victor Frankl, "Beyond Self-Actualization and Self Expression," *Journal of Existential ychiatry 1,* No. 1 (Spring 1960): 5–20.

ism develops according to its innate pattern and in that sense you could say that it is a process that is largely determined, partly by genetic factors and partly by the environment. I think all of that is true in man as well, but for me the element that changes that situation in the human being is the development of consciousness or awareness, and consequently it would be insufficient to talk just in terms of actualization.

Frick: Or the innate kinds of things?

Rogers: Yes. I've always made a distinction here. I don't know whether I've always carried this through but I do recall trying to clarify the distinction in this way. I'd be perfectly willing to speak about *actualization* of the human organism which I think follows the same kind of lawful process that you find in any living organism. But I think *self-actualization* does have reference to something a little more than that, which does grow out of a person's awareness. . . .

Frick: The conscious component.

Rogers: That's right, the conscious component or the conscious and potentially conscious component. In that area I am a hearty believer in the fact that not only does the individual choose many elements of himself, and in that sense creates himself, but I believe that is one of the most distinctive things about the human organism which does tend to separate it off from other forms of life.

Frick: This is, then, a part of his genetic makeup in a sense, the power to choose.

Rogers: Yes, part of his genetic makeup that grows out of the fact that in his evolution he has developed consciousness and awareness and consequently, as far as we know, he is the only animal who really can be aware of his past as well as his present and consequently can make some choices about his future.

Frick: I guess to make this more specific in terms of my quandary here, which is personal as well as academic, I always ask myself the question in reading the theoretical material on self-actualization "Does the organism have the freedom to choose between good and evil?" and somehow it seems to me that the self-actualizing theorists including your work, answer "no" to this question. If conditions are ripe or adequate for the human organism there seems to

Chapter 3

be the idea that man will *automatically* do those goo
as a part of his inherent nature. That is, he really doesn .
tween good and evil. He is on a kind of automatic pilot ι,
tions are good. Is that a fair evaluation?

Rogers: Yes, I think I would go along with that but I would certainly underscore that final phrase you use, "if conditions are
good," by which I would mean if the conditions are such as to promote healthy growth, then I think you can trust the choices of the
individual to be social but it's very obvious from all kinds of things
that are going on in the world today that for many people the conditions of growth and development have been far from those that
promote a healthy development. So you get destructive choices,
you get some enormous amounts of aggression, you get all sorts of
things that we would regard as socially undesirable and man is perfectly capable of making these choices when his situation has not
been good and, again, when he's not been fully aware of himself
and his background. I don't know whether you know a little paper
of mine that was written many years ago with Bill Kell and Helen
McNeil.[2] It was based on some research that Bill Kell did under my
supervision and was a study of delinquents and their further delin-
quencies. By studying the case histories of the delinquents, he rated
them on various factors: the goodness or badness of their genetic in-
heritance, their intelligence, their family background, their social
environment, and then as sort of an afterthought we put in a rating
on self-understanding and we assumed, at least my own assumption
was, that what we would find was that probably the family environment would be most predictive of recidivism. What actually turned
out, and we really didn't believe it the first time, was that the degree of self-understanding correlated much more with the future.
That is, a person with relatively good understanding of himself and
his situation, a relatively realistic appreciation of that, was far less
likely to become delinquent, and that just seemed too good to be
true. At that time I wasn't prepared to believe that finding. We
didn't publish this because I just didn't believe it. Sometime later
Helen McNeil did the same study over again with a new crop of

[2] C. R. Rogers, B. L. Kell, and H. McNeil, "The Role of Self-Understanding in the Prediction of Behavior," *Journal of Consulting Psychology* 12 (1948), 174–186.

elinquents with not quite as striking findings as Bill Kell had gotten, but essentially all the same things. That's why I stress the importance of real awareness and especially a realistic awareness of self and one's situation in choosing the future.

✿   ✿   ✿   ✿   ✿

Frick: Dr. Rogers, at various times in your writings you have implied an acceptance of Maslow's instinctoid need hierarchy and yet you have stated in one of your recent writings that you felt that love, the need for love, is learned. This seems a little bit inconsistent of you and it bothered me when I ran across that statement. I'm wondering if you care to comment on this?

Rogers: I guess it's been quite a while since I've thought about that issue and I'm a little bit puzzled to know whether I said that. Perhaps this appeared in the Koch book,[3] because at that time I was influenced by some theoretical thinking that one of my students was doing. I think I would have to say that the need for love and affection seems to me to be innate and if I have said anything that would contradict that, I think I would probably go back on it.

Frick: Well, it has been a number of years since you wrote that material in Koch.

Rogers: Yes, much earlier than when it was published. I think it was written about 1953. I think Harlow's work indicates that even in non-human organisms the need for affection seems pretty deep and I would think that would be true with the human being, too.

✿   ✿   ✿   ✿   ✿

congruence

Frick: I have one other question, Dr. Rogers, that deals with the issue of determinism here and it is related to your concept of congruence. This is one of the key concepts that you have been working with. Do you feel that the person is a victim, in the deterministic sense, of the conditions of worth that are placed upon him by others? Cannot he ignore certain conditions of worth, reject them, or say "to hell with them." Maslow suggests this when he speaks of the healthy person as being able to transcend the cultu:

---

[3] Carl R. Rogers, "A Theory of Therapy, Personality and Interpersonal Relationships Developed in the Client-Centered Framework," in *Psychology: A Study of a Science*, V III., ed. S. Koch (New York: McGraw-Hill, 1959.)

or the society by refusing to accept certain values and impo
I wonder if the child is as victimized by conditions of worth
seem to suggest in your theory of congruence. Isn't it possi
the young person to say "This is not the way it is and I reject the
conditions you're imposing on me, mother, in order for me to feel
worthy."

Rogers: Yes, I think the clearest example of the fact that that is
possible is the kind of thing that happens continually in psychotherapy where a person is saying, "Yes, I was thought to be no
good, but, by God, as I really look at myself and examine my experience, I have confidence. I have a lot of positive qualities and I'm
just *not* going to accept that evaluation." I think that *can* happen in
a child. . . .

Frick: Outside of therapy?

Rogers: Yes. I think that can happen in various individuals outside
of therapy. By and large I think there is no doubt that it is easier for
the person to reject conditions of worth when he has not been subjected to a great many of them; that is, the individual who is already weighed down with all kinds of things very early in life. I
think he would find it very difficult to reject those conditions without some sort of help, some sort of a therapeutic climate, whether it
was planned or unplanned. I think probably the more psychologically healthy the development of the child, the more he
would be able to challenge conditions of worth.

Frick: Dr. Rogers, you have often insisted that the state of congruence equals psychological adjustment or psychological health.
Now, I've been wondering if it's not possible for a person to be in a
very high state of congruence and still be a disturbed personality.
Does the condition or state of congruence insure healthy personal-
ty? In other words, I can see people that I regard as being very
congruent and yet I wouldn't regard them as healthy. This seems to
me to be rather important because you do equate the state of congruence with health.

Rogers: Well, you have obviously been thinking more about these
issues than I have recently. I get theoretical by spurts, and it has
been some time since I really have buckled down to hard theo-
etical thinking. That's why I wondered at the outset if I could get

in a theoretical mood. I don't think I'll attempt any definitive answer to that. I'll just try to think out loud a little bit about it. One
thought that occurs to me is that if the individual is experiencing
something in his organism, if he's aware of it in himself, aware of it
and acceptant enough of that experiencing that he even would be
able to express it if the situation was appropriate for it, then I think
I would say that he is in as great a degree of psychological health as
his organism would permit at that moment. Something of that sort I
think I would be willing to stand by. Take someone who is over-
whelmed by grief, or someone who is very much conflicted in
thinking about some choice or some aspect of his life. I think the
more an individual is fully aware of what's going on within him at
that point, the more he is making as healthy a reaction to that situation as is possible.

Frick: I guess what I'm saying is that it seems to me that congruence can represent a kind of static state, a state of ennui or bore-
dom and I go back to Maslow's recent discovery that just because
the basic deficiency needs are met, it does not automatically mean
that the person is going to reach a level of self-actualization. Prior
to this he has always assumed that once these deficiency needs have
been fully satisfied the person automatically moves into a higher
level of functioning or self-actualizing stage. I guess that's what
made me think of the state of congruence as not being a sufficient
condition for health.

Rogers: Let me talk off the top of my head on that. I don't think I
could agree that congruence could be a state of ennui or apathy because I think things are always going on in the human organism
There couldn't be anything static about congruence because one's
experience is continually changing and to be really congruen
would mean a continually changing awareness. The other aspect to
your question is as to whether an individual is automatically self-ac
tualizing. I guess I would have to confess to being uncertain. No
perhaps I feel more certain than I recognize. I think there do have
to be various stimulus situations around. I say this partly on th
basis of a very practical observation that I made when I was visitin
Australia and New Zealand, that many of the conditions for an ade
quate life are very well fulfilled; the physical needs are met an
there really is almost nothing that you would call poverty and ne

ther is there anything very extreme in the way of wealth. Their physical needs are pretty adequately met and they're secure in their medical care, in their lifetime care, and so on. And, instead of those conditions leading to a utopia, it's a fairly dull society. In Australia you could see that sort of breaking down a little as they've been taking in recent immigrants, trying to import them from Europe. People are being stimulated to new thoughts and new opportunities and new possibilities. I think probably we can make a parallel between this and the school child too, that you could meet his physical needs very well, and still perhaps he wouldn't be very much of a learning organism. You do have to surround him with stimulating opportunities for learning and development and then I think he eats them up. I see it more as the presence of external stimulation.

Frick: Yes. You know, I think they have said the same thing about the Scandanavian countries that you observed in New Zealand and Australia. Everyone is apparently so secure, and yet there are real problems and the young are still restless. I am wondering if this doesn't really take us back to education. That is, the need to stimulate at some very basic levels here. I don't think education is really doing this.

Rogers: No, I don't either.

Frick: Education is still stuck at the cognitive level and with the three R's and I'm wondering if children really are getting the kind of stimulations that Gardner Murphy would talk about, leading them to cosmic consciousness, or something similar at their level of development.[4] They are such rich, creative people at that age.

Rogers: Well, that's an issue I feel very strongly about, because I think that as an institution education is the most backward of any in American life. I've got a new book coming out in a month or so now, entitled *Freedom to Learn*,[5] where one of the things that I *do* try to stress is the importance of a much greater freedom for the individual and not all this—what do they call it—mug and jug theory where they pour from the mug into the jug, which I think describes too much of education today. The child may be given a

---

[4] Gardner Murphy, *Human Potentialities* (New York: Basic Books, Inc., 1958).
[5] Carl Rogers, *Freedom To Learn* (Columbus, Ohio: Charles Merrill Publishing Co., 1969).

great deal of freedom to learn but then freedom to learn in a vacuum is not profitable. This is why I make the point in that book that if teachers devoted as much time to thinking about the learning resources they could make available to these children, or to students at any level, as they do with the contents of the next lecture, we could surround students at all levels with very rich opportunities from which they could choose . . . and where they could learn and learn at their own pace and consequently with a lot of personal satisfaction. I guess I'm not quite so concerned about cosmic consciousness as I am about the individual developing some new and significant channel for himself that would carry him beyond. . . .

Frick: That draws upon his own potential.

Rogers: That's right. That gives him an opportunity for creativity and where he goes further than he ever has before in whatever direction.

Frick: I'm wondering, Dr. Rogers, if you think this has some pertinent bearing on the drug abuse that we're seeing young people involved in today. Our attacks at this problem seem so peripheral. Do you think this would have a bearing on their experimenting with drugs?

Rogers: Oh, definitely. One reason I'm so interested at the present time in encounter groups and the intensive group experience is that I feel that when people have an opportunity to use themselves fully and to relate on both an affective and cognitive basis to others, to themselves, to a world of facts and discoveries, etc., that they do get turned on and they get turned on quite without drugs, and I think they find it—and I would certainly regard it—as a far more constructive way of getting turned on than drugs. I think that the use of drugs is increasing especially among high school students and is due to a number of things. It is a rebellion against a society with stupid values, but I think it is also a rebellion against a stupid, so-called learning environment that *isn't* a learning environment.

Frick: It is the lack of stimulation in other ways, perhaps. You know, I was sitting in the beautiful La Jolla Cove yesterday and it was just a beautiful scene. The waves were breaking over the rocks and it was magnificent and then I looked around and saw the houses on the hillside and I got to thinking what a discrepancy this is in

terms of the way so many people are living their l̶ [96]
very sad and somehow, you know, it was out of focus̶

Rogers: The possibilities are so rich and the actua̶
poverished.

Frick: That's right, and then I thought that really the La J̶o̶̶
Cove represents something very basic to man that he has somehow
lost touch with, I think.

Rogers: That is something that has real meaning for me. I think it's
terribly unfortunate that man has tended to lose touch with external nature in so many instances, as well as with his own internal nature, and between the two of them he is a very alienated organism
existing in a world that doesn't exist.

Frick: That's right, and I think I'm going to refer back to Gardner
Murphy again here because I think this is something he's done. He
has tried to link the external environment with the internal needs of
the human organism. It relates to your comment on education, I
think, because this is what you would like to see education do, in
part.

Rogers: Yes, that's right.

      ✿   ✿   ✿   ✿   ✿

Frick: I would like to take up a question dealing with holistic theory, Dr. Rogers. In my study of the holistic personality theorists I
have isolated or discerned two primary themes of holistic personality theory. One of them is the drive of the personality for self-consistency or organization, bringing completion to an incomplete
structure. The second major theme stresses the evolution of the personality, viewing the personality as always in process, in flux, and
undergoing change at all times. It seems to me that there are certain conflicts in these two holistic themes and I would like to talk
about them for a few minutes. I don't know whether you recognize
them or not. Maslow has suggested that the need for safety is prepotent over the organism's growth needs and Prescott Lecky's entire reputation rests on that one little book he wrote, *Self Consistency*.[6] I think this question could be approached in many
different ways but if number one is true, that is, if the organism

---

[6] Prescott Lecky, *Self-Consistency* (New York: Island Press, 1945).

…oes strive for organization, stability, cohesiveness, and a well-structured kind of development in the personality, what accounts for change and growth and becoming? I do see a conflict here in these two themes and I think we need to tie them together theoretically. I would like you to comment and then I have a suggestion.

Rogers: I think that is a very discerning distinction you have made. Some of the thoughts that come to me first have to do with therapy or experiences in small groups, where I've often said—and certainly feel—that any significant learning, and I guess by significant learning I mean learning that might influence one's behavior, is to some degree threatening. If I'm about to learn something that might change my picture of myself, or the way in which I react to situations, that's upsetting. All significant learning tends to involve a certain amount of threat and pain, I think, from very mild to sometimes quite severe. It is a good question, and I'm interested in whatever answer you may have to the dilemma because I think that both of those things are very true. Why does a child learn to walk? It's really a very interesting and paradoxical question. He tries to stand up and he falls and bumps his head. Learning to walk is a painful proposition. There's certainly no great reward to it until he really makes the grade and yet he's willing to go through that pain as a part of a biologically based process. . . .

Frick: Even when he knows his parent will pick him up if he stretches his arms.

Rogers: That's right. To me, that is a capsule indication that unless the learning involves such a drastic reorganization that it is just too threatening and the person can't face it at all, there is a real drawing power to the possibility of further growth.

Frick: The possibility for constructive change.

Rogers: Yes, change. And I think that's what we bank on really. Certainly, you see this operating in small groups where an individual takes some pretty tough feedback from other members of the group and, boy, he's really hurting from that. Why, then, doesn't he just leave the group and forget what they said? No, if he has any feeling that this might lead to some sort of constructive change on his part, he hangs in there with the difficulties and lives through them, and is glad afterwards. I remember one specific incident that has always been rather meaningful to me. A woman—she was the only woman in a group of business executives and she was an executive herself—talked a little in the group about how much she was dominated by her mother, but I didn't realize that she had come to any significant conclusions during the group meetings. Afterward, though, she went home and took some quite drastic steps. She found an apartment for her mother and moved her mother into it so that they were separated and the mother wept and felt quite rejected. Yet the mother soon adjusted to her new life as she was a pretty independent person. This forty year old woman discovered that *she* was the problem. She wasn't prepared to be independent. She really went through continuing agony and kept writing me letters during this period. Finally I wrote back to her and said, "I'll bet there are plenty of times when you wish you had never heard of that damn group that has opened up such a lot of pain for you." Her response was the kind of response that human beings make. She wrote back and said, "No. You're right that this has been the most painful period of my life, but I wouldn't have avoided it for anything." The possibility of further maturity and of constructive change must have a real magnetic attraction. That's the closest I come to linking the two together.

Frick: Yes, I have been struggling with this kind of conflict, the individual striving to protect a valued status versus the need to grow. And it seems to me in some of the recent work and writing that has been done, the concept of crisis is more and more appealing as a conceptual bridge between the striving for organization and unity versus the need for personality change. Are you familiar with Dabrowski's book on *Positive Disintegration?*[7]

Rogers: No, I'm not, but I like that phrase.

Frick: It's really quite an exciting book. And Menninger has a section in his recent book, *The Vital Balance,*[8] where he uses brief case histories to illustrate the tremendous changes that have come about in certain people because of crisis. Even mental illness is viewed as a potentially positive experience. I can't find any more appealing concept than crisis to bridge the conflict in these two

[7] Kazimierz Dabrowski, *Positive Disintegration* (Boston: Little, Brown & Co., 1964).
[8] Karl Menninger, *The Vital Balance* (New York: The Viking Press, 1963), p. 406–417.

themes. I am wondering if the most significant growth in people doesn't emerge out of crisis situations. We see it in therapy, but I wonder if it also isn't true outside therapy.

Rogers: I think so. I think anything that's true in therapy is also true outside of therapy. I like that concept and it would be pretty well illustrated by the story I just gave you. Also, it fits in with what I said earlier about the fact that external stimulation is necessary. That is, the crisis usually comes about, in part, because of some external circumstance and that would make real sense to me. Also in my mind it fits in with what I said about the New Zealanders. There are just not sufficient crises in their lives, to put it in your terms. This can have very sobering implications. Goodness knows I'm all in favor of all our efforts to improve the lot of the people, and yet I have come to realize that a life without tension would be no good.

Frick: That reminds me, Dr. Rogers, that as I toured San Diego yesterday, I thought about how many things we saw that highlighted man's effort to make life safe, easy, and secure and the anxious efforts to protect the upward mobile strivings. It was just all over and really shocking to confront. I'm wondering, and here we go back to education, if there is a way to put stimulus into life, to put crisis in, maybe a controlled crisis in some way.

Rogers: I don't know if this will get us too far afield but it relates to a recent experience I had dealing with groups from Columbia University—trustees and administrators and faculty and students. One of the students was making some pretty extreme statements including the fact that buildings might burn. One of the trustees responded with a very well-reasoned, very carefully thought-out defense of the proposition that all difficulties in the end have to be settled through rational discourse, and that that was really the answer, and that violence certainly was not part of it. The students just mowed him down. I really was impressed. They said "Why are we here this weekend? Because of rational discourse? It's because we occupied buildings last May. Why is Grayson Kirk out as President of Columbia? Rational discourse? Hell no. It's because we created a fuss." And they just went through a whole long list of things that showed that . . .

Frick: They knew the value of crises, didn't they?

Rogers: Yes, they certainly did. I just hope they don't overlearn that lesson or we'll be repeating the French Revolution where violence was very constructive and then gradually fed on itself until the means became the end.

Frick: Dr. Rogers, were you called in as a consultant at Columbia?

Rogers: Yes, I was. I was one of several staff members experienced in small group activity and in part of this experience all 70 people were together and part of the time we were in small, intensive groups. There was one other thing I came away with. Of all the different groups that were there, the most difficult to reach was the *faculty*. I really came away feeling that we made some dent on the total group in the communicated inter-change, but I also came away feeling quite pessimistic because I felt that the faculty were, by and large, too smug, not sufficiently open to experience, and making absurd statements like, "We have good communication with students. We talk with students all the time."

Frick: In the face of what's going on, they say this.

Rogers: Yes, and it seemed to me that, as the phrase goes, they were applying band-aids when things like that were perfectly inadequate and seemingly without any recognition that what they were facing was revolution.

Frick: It's sad.

Rogers: Yes, very, very sad. Of course, I'm generalizing. This wouldn't be true of all the faculty members who were there. But by and large I thought they were the group that would be the greatest barrier. One of the students said something to me that also applies to our discussion this morning and to all theoretical thinking. He said that it seemed to him there were two worlds here, and he wasn't at all sure that the two could ever really communicate. He was thinking about the students and the adults. He said one big difference, perhaps one of the most important differences, is that the student world contains *feelings*. To me he really said a mouthful, because I think that all of our academic life has been built on the notion of the completely cognitive, the completely intellectual, and that was one of the reasons why the faculty were *so* hard to reach. The world of feelings for a great many of them just doesn't exist. And to tie it in with this discussion this morning, there is one thing I wanted to be sure to say before we got through. I have very mixed feelings about theory building. I think that's why it does go in spurts for me. There are times when, for myself, I need to try to make some sense out of a whole lot of experience, and so what comes out of that is a theory. I mean, you develop some sort of theory to . . .

Frick: But you can't live on that, can you?

Rogers: You can't live on that, and also I even wonder . . . It *is* satisfying and you feel, well, now I have that clearer than I had it before. I begin to see what's been happening, or what some of the process elements are. But I sometimes wonder if all theories shouldn't be kept to oneself, because theory gets promulgated—especially with students—as being "This is the way things are," or "This is the way expert number one says they are, and this is the way expert number two says they are, so it must be one of those two ways." The value of theory exists, I think, in its construction and not in its dissemination. Quite possibly you could make out a case that the dissemination of theory does more harm than good. But the *construction* of theory, that's a very rewarding experience for the individual. And I'd like to see part of education providing the kind of stimulus that would create at least a small internal crisis by encouraging such questions as: "How could all these things be true, or what could possibly make sense out of all this confusion of facts and observations?"

Frick: You would like to wipe away the slate of theory and encourage a fresh look?

Rogers: That's right and then the student would have to start to figure out, "Well, what do *I* think makes sense out of this?" even though his theories were crude and incomplete and so on. He would get a great deal from the experience.

Frick: He would get involved. This is interesting to hear you say after all you've had to do with theory building, Dr. Rogers.

Rogers: It's interesting—I mean, let me say just one word about that because I don't really think of myself as a theoretician. It is true that for a couple of years when I was working on what became the Koch chapter, that was a very strenuous effort on my part to make some sense out of all my professional experience and personal experience up to that point.[9] But as I have watched what people do with my theories and what they do with other people's theories, God! I remember I wrote Calvin Hall after his book on Theories of Personality[10] came out. They were kind enough to send me the chapter in regard to my theory in advance of publication, and I guess I hurt their feelings by writing back that, "I wouldn't say that there were many misstatements of fact in the chapter, it's just that reading the whole thing left me terribly depressed." It left me terribly depressed because here was everything all cut and dried, and hell, it had never seemed that way to me. It would seem as though, well, out of all the possibilities this might be one possible explanation. But no, when it comes out, especially second hand like that, it is all a nicely packaged thing with everything closed.

Frick: The struggle is left out completely, isn't it? You know, Ledford Bischof has written a recent book on personality theory, *Interpreting Personality Theory.*[11] I was amused that somewhere in the chapter on your theory he comes right out and says that you disagree with his interpretation.

✿   ✿   ✿   ✿   ✿

Dr. Rogers, in the recent book, *Beyond Counseling and Therapy* by Carkhuff and Berenson,[12] there is a critique of client-centered psychotherapy. I don't know whether you are familiar with this book or not.

Rogers: I really haven't read it. I do know about it though.

Frick: I think it's an excellent book and feel that they've made a real contribution. One of the chief limitations they see in the client-centered approach is the client-centered therapist's lack of freedom to be a whole and spontaneous person in relation to the client. In this regard they state: "Client-centered therapy brought more complete attention to the whole person of the client, but has neglected

[9] Rogers, "A Theory of Therapy," in *Psychology*, ed. S. Koch.

[10] Calvin Hall and Gardner Lindzey, *Theories of Personality* (New York: John Wiley and Sons, Inc., 1957).

[11] Ledford J. Bischof, *Interpreting Personality Theories* (New York: Harper and Row, 1964).

[12] Robert R. Carkhuff and Bernard G. Berenson, *Beyond Counseling and Therapy* (New York: Holt, Rinehart, and Winston, Inc., 1967).

the *whole person of the therapist,* and the two-way flow of communication." [13] Dr. Rogers, there does seem to be an increasing emphasis on the freedom of the therapist to do his own thing; to be more spontaneous, more wide-ranging in his efforts to help the client, and perhaps existential therapy has come in here to influence this, I don't know, but do you agree in part with this criticism that client-centered therapy *has* neglected the whole person of the therapist?

Rogers: I would say that as of 1950 I would agree with them completely. I think that following that time there has been a gradual change in just the direction they're talking about with the therapist much more free to use and be himself as a whole person in the relationship, and for me personally . . . how will I say it . . . the trial ground for this development has been more in work with groups, for reasons I don't fully understand, but I'm sure that if I were to go back to doing individual therapy, which I haven't been able to do for some years, I am sure I would be much more free in expressing my own feelings and my spontaneous self in a relationship as well as trying to help the client be the same.

Frick: You say that you do this in work with groups?

Rogers: Oh, yes, definitely. I express anger, and affection, and annoyance and all kinds of things, as well as being very responsive to hurt. Hurt arouses in me feelings of really wanting to be empathic so that a lot of the therapeutic attitudes that I've stressed, I think, are very real parts of me, and of many therapists, and so they need expression as well, but other feelings, too, have equal validity.

Frick: You have gone beyond these limitations suggested by Carkhuff and Berenson, then?

Rogers: Yes, definitely. And then I think . . . Well, I was reading a paper the other day written by Hilding Carlson over at San Diego State. It was sort of a personal account of his own development as a counselor, and I couldn't help but write him a letter afterward because he had been greatly influenced by the client-centered point of view, and now feels that he has gone beyond it, and primarily in this direction of being more of a complete person in the relation-

---

[13] Ibid., p. 68.

rogers — move beyond client centered therapy (handwritten)

ship. I wrote him that it was fascinating to me how we all develop along parallel lines, because his work, what might be called a "Client-Centered Therapist as in 1950," left him dissatisfied and he's moved on beyond that and so have I, and so . . .

Frick: Kind of independently.

Rogers: Yes. Even though he's here in the same community we have had almost no contact for quite a number of years, and this is what I find time and again. I think, "Well, I've certainly changed, but now I'm going to meet someone that I knew ten years ago, and they're probably still back where they were," but they've moved along the same lines.

Frick: Well, you know, the same thing has happened to me too. I have done quite a bit of counseling with college students, and I've shifted over a period of time in my orientation as well as an increased feeling of freedom in approaching clients.

Rogers: While I was still at the University of Chicago *Time* magazine did an article on me and Client-Centered Therapy, and like all *Time* articles, I read it and thought that, well, they got some of the idea, and some of this is pretty good, and some of it is typically *Time*. I was telling this to someone and they said, "Well, they gave you an excellent term," and I asked, "What do you mean?" They said, "The title of the thing . . ." and I asked, "What was it? I guess I haven't looked at it that closely." They said, "It was labeled 'Person to Person Therapy.'" "By gosh," I said, "that's true." That really is perhaps the best term for it, because that phrase certainly catches much more . . . I have never known who coined the word "non-directive." If I did, I apologize for it, but at any rate that certainly was descriptive of a certain early phase. Later the emphasis was on the client's perceptions, and therefore *client*-centered. The term has been often misunderstood, but it was supposed to represent the thought that this therapy was focused on the client's perception of his life and his problems. I don't think any label has been given to the further development, but certainly "Person to Person Therapy" would be a very good label.

* * * * *

Dr. Rogers, we've seen a great increase in the popularity . . . almost a faddish kind of interest in behavior therapy, and from another direction we have an emphasis upon the existential approaches to human relationships and problem solving. Elsewhere in the theoretical spectrum we have client-centered or non-directive therapy and other approaches as well. I'm wondering, Dr. Rogers, what you see taking place in psychotherapy in the next few years, and what the trends in psychotherapy really reflect about a society. It seems to me that the fashions in psychotherapy are pretty crucial in mirroring certain things about a society. Could you make that case, or not? What would it mean about our society, for example, if behavior therapy zooms to the forefront of the various therapeutic approaches with people? Do you know what I mean?

Rogers: Sure.

Frick: And I'm wondering what your responses are to this, your predictions, and so on.

Rogers: I hadn't quite thought of therapy as mirroring the society and the trends in it, but I think a good case could probably be made for that. As I see it, I would really predict that there would be a sharp upward rise in the use of behavior therapy, because I think that fits in with the thinking of a great majority of psychologists which, oversimplified, could be stated as being that man is a complicated machine, but we can probably understand him and control him. I think that's part of the mood of present-day culture, and that's why I would see behavior therapy as likely to increase. On the other hand, the attitudes of young people make me feel that the days of that point of view are numbered. The behavioristic kind of psychology is very much in the saddle in universities and what with tenure and all, it will be a long time before the universities really change. But I don't believe that the younger generation coming along will be satisfied with that kind of a view of life and I think that the existential point of view, which means many different things to many different people, is going to be predominant. Certainly my version of this point of view has a great deal of meaning to me, and I think that . . . no, I guess this is more of a hope than an assurance. I *hope* that the humanistic person-to-person communication, which has really been shown to be possible, will play a larger and larger part, but I would have to say that that probably is a hope rather than a sure prediction! That's the horse I'm betting on for the long run. And I don't mean to separate it from existentialism, because I don't really think there's a contradiction.

Frick: But I think there is a *basic* contradiction with the theoretical orientation we see in behavior therapy. You could gloss that over if you wanted to, but I think there are fundamental differences in how they perceive man as compared to you, as compared to the humanists.

Rogers: That's right.

Frick: And, Dr. Rogers, if you *do* see behavior therapy playing a larger role here, I feel there's something wrong about that in society. Because this means more and more people are accepting it, more and more clients are accepting it, and more and more treatment facilities are accepting it and, frankly, this seems to me to be kind of a regression.

Rogers: Oh, I think so too. For me, this goes back to the debate I had with Skinner. That didn't involve therapy, particularly, but the two basic differences are still existent. I like to think that at some point . . . let's see, how shall I put this . . . I wouldn't like to discard the obvious significance which operant conditioning and all that sprung from it, has for human life and human behavior. It's more than interesting, it has . . .

Frick: It's a real contribution.

Rogers: Yes, and yet if that becomes the be all and end all, and particularly if that becomes the philosophical point of view which dominates, I would regard that as tragic. At some point I hope that someone can bridge the humanistic-existential point of view and the strictly behaviorist point of view into one more over-arching way of seeing the human world. But . . .

Frick: That doesn't seem likely does it? I mean, I can't see that . . .

Rogers: Well, I think historically it sounds likely and probable, but I don't really observe it happening. The reason I say that it is historically probable is that most theories don't get killed, especially when they've been as effective as the behaviorist theories, but they do get assimilated into something larger with a broader perspective, and I hope that will be what will happen.

Frick: This leads me to an article that you wrote some time ago in the *Journal of Humanistic Psychology* [14] where you were somewhat pessimistic about what the Association for Humanistic Psychology and this whole movement was going to be able to do. You pointed out that it was one thing to be critical of existing theories and approaches, but it was entirely another thing to make a positive contribution. This article was written several years ago, and I would like to know if you see this humanistic movement in psychology making more of a positive contribution now, or do you still feel it's more a reactive kind of phase?

Rogers: I guess that I would stress that what I'm going to say is strictly from an individual perspective. I feel as though I don't know what's happening in the humanistic movement, really. Somebody would have to be more of an observer than I am. I am a person who is involved in what I am doing. At any rate, from my own personal perspective, I think that the humanistic trends, among psychologists and others with similar interests, are finding many positive things, and I think they are engaged in them. And I would certainly put the burgeoning of the small group experience as one of those attempts to deal with human alienation and inter-personal communication and many problems and situations that have real implications for the individual human being. So that I do think there are a number of positive things being done. And then along with that I guess, I'd put the increasing questioning of the whole concept of science as it has been used in the behavioral sciences. I don't know whether you've seen that new book that Bill Coulson and I edited that grew out of a conference that we organized here, and centered around Michael Polanyi, the British philosopher of science.[15]

Frick: No, I haven't seen that book.

Rogers: I guess if I were to try to sum it up in a sentence, that conference—which contained it's own conflicts because there was a very strong behaviorist in the group, as well as people with different shades of philosophical opinion—constitutes one of the evidences of the very significant groping that's taking place toward

[14] Carl R. Rogers, "Some Questions and Challenges Facing A Humanistic Psychology," *Journal of Humanistic Psychology* Vol. V, No. 1 (Spring 1965).
[15] Carl Rogers and William Coulson, *Man and the Science of Man* (Columbus, Ohio: Charles E. Merrill Publishing Co., 1968).

some type of human science. I think psychology, especially university psychology, is really living by an outdated model of science.
They are going by a Newtonian concept of science that I think is
definitely out of date. I think they have never faced the problems
created by the scientist being both the scientist and the material of
his science. It's something that no other science has really had to
face, because it's just been a little peripheral problem that the human factor does enter into the reading of the dial or the photograph
or whatever, even in the "hardest" of the physical sciences. But
where you are not only the subject but the *object* of the science as
well, it creates a great many new problems. I believe we have not
yet found what science might mean as applied to the human being.
One other statement on that and then I'll sign off. As you can see,
it's something I'm quite interested in. When Michael Polanyi first
said to me that he wished we'd quit using the term "science" for at
least a decade and just think about acquiring knowledge, I really
was unsympathetic to that statement. Gradually, however, I've
come to agree with him quite completely. I wish that in the behavioral field, in the human field, we could forget all about *science*,
which for psychologists is all methodology—and that isn't what it is
among the real scientists in harder fields—if we could forget all
about that and just ask ourselves "How could we acquire more
knowledge about human beings?" That knowledge might be useful,
it might even be interchangeable. That is, you and I might see the
same thing, or gain the same kind of experience from a given situation. I think we would be much better off because then we would
be free to be creative about our approach to problems.

Frick: Well, this might bring about a rapprochement between behavior therapy and the other approaches, you know.

Rogers: Yes, I think so.

✿   ✿   ✿   ✿   ✿

Frick: Dr. Rogers, you have made the point that truth is never a
closed and finished book, and I would like to quote you here:
"There will be new discoveries which will contradict the best theories which we can construct . . ." This statement appeared in your
paper in the Koch book.[16] Now, my question is this: What do you
regard as the most likely or promising theoretical changes in your

[16] Rogers, "A Theory of Therapy," in *Psychology*, ed. S. Koch, p. 190.

theory, to get theoretical again? Do you see any signs of things taking place that might be changing your theories quite a bit, or do you have that perspective now?

Rogers: Of course, if I really knew the answer to that I could be launching out on new theories, and new aspects of theory myself, so all I can do is just speculate a little bit on what are probably some peripheral things. I can't quite say what specific changes might occur, but I think that by utilizing even more than I have the internal world of the individual as the base for theoretical thinking, that probably would bring a significantly changed emphasis into the theories, because one thing I know that I have vaguely felt about various attempts of mine to organize things theoretically, is that there is a strong temptation, then, to externalize it.

Frick: Yes, I've noticed this in some of your writings.

Rogers: For instance in therapy, I really rely on the internal world of the other individual. That's the thing that teaches me, out of which I learn, but I don't think I've ever known well enough how one could construct a theory from that vantage point. And maybe that is quite important. One other small thing would be to repeat what I've been saying that I probably would make less effort to build a theory on empirical evidence. I can't be accused of overdoing that, certainly, but I did try to bring in as much empirical evidence as I could, particularly in the Koch theory statement. I guess I would play down somewhat the importance of that, because I think that our empirical attempts in the psychological field are really so primitive that they're damned near useless, and . . .

Frick: . . . worse than useless sometimes, perhaps.

Rogers: Yes, and perhaps profound insights growing out of immersion in the phenomena, in this case the phenomena of human living or becoming a person or whatever, would be definitely preferable to trying to back up any observations with empirical data.

¤   ¤   ¤   ¤   ¤

Frick: Dr. Rogers, I read the article that you wrote outlining a plan for using T-groups or the sensitivity training methods to change an entire educational system, to bring about innovation in education. At the end of the article you asked if there were any takers of your proposal. After I finished reading the article I wondered how many expressed serious interest or real commitment to your ideas.[17]

Rogers: Oh, the response to that was very interesting. Quite a number of school systems said, "We'd like to be the school system in which you work," but they really didn't have the funds for that. One foundation executive wrote me immediately after he had read it and he said, "You bet you've got a taker. We'll put this a little bit more in proposal form and we'll give you backing." And then to his enormous embarrassment his Board of Trustees wouldn't go along with it. It was too far out for them. It had already been turned down by one or two foundations and the Office of Education turned it down twice. But then another foundation heard about it, got interested in it, and they did give us backing. One reason I haven't been much involved in theory in the last couple of years, is that I became very much immersed in doing this, trying to carry out that plan.

Frick: What school system is this now, Dr. Rogers?

Rogers: I had assumed that, of course, it would be a public school system and there were a number of public school systems not too far from here who were very eager to be the target system. Then we had some visitors from the Immaculate Heart Order and they wanted the educational system of their Order to be the target system and I said no. I thought it should be a public school system and besides, I really didn't think that parochial schools were up to the level of public high schools. But gradually, there were several factors that made us choose the parochial system. For one thing, it was the only one with a college that was turning out teachers so we could deal with the college level too. There were also eight high schools and fifty elementary schools, so it was really a pretty whopping system to tackle, and we've had a most fascinating year and a half at it.

Frick: Are you actually involved in group contact yourself, or are you involved in supervising the . . .

Rogers: The way I like to work on something like that, since I

---

[17] Carl Rogers, "A Plan for Self-Directed Change in an Educational System." Mimeographed and distributed by the author, 27 pages.

don't like administration of any kind, is to get someone who will serve as administrator to the project. I like to be in at the grass roots level, and then at the conceptual and writing up level and that's what I've done. I've worked with groups of faculty and administrators, and recently a group of administrators of the college, and a group of high school girls, and high school faculty and students. These two groups finally were willing to get together, not initially, but they got to the point where they decided they wouldn't be too dangerous to each other, and there again, it was the faculty who were frightened, not the students.

Frick: They're the rigid ones, aren't they?

Rogers: They're the rigid ones. And then I've dealt with faculties of elementary schools and I've been carrying on a lot of the groups myself.

Frick: This is kind of surprising, Dr. Rogers, that this would turn out to be a Catholic school system.

Rogers: Yes, well, they are a very surprising set-up. Certainly at the elementary school level, and perhaps at the college level too, perhaps all the way through they are more consistently forward-looking than any educational system I've known. They are really a very swinging group. I don't know whether you've come across this in newspapers, but because they took some quite modern stands like deciding not to wear their habit and a number of things that went against the traditional notions, Cardinal McIntyre shut them out of all the elementary schools, so that these elementary schools that we worked with are now no longer available to us, which sounds quite tragic, but I don't feel too badly about it because the people whom we've dealt with have gone into other schools and . . .

Frick: . . . you mean the people you were working with?

Rogers: Yes, they really were dropped from all of the 50 elementary schools that were under his jurisdiction. There might be a few that were not. The Sisters were put out of them.

Frick: Well, this really destroyed your plan in those schools, didn't it?

Rogers: It did as far as those schools are concerned, yes, but I say the reason I don't regard it as a tragedy, is that we had an awfully good experience and saw some of the changes taking place before they were put out. Then the second thing that makes me feel comfortable about it is that all of those people that we affected, after all, have gone into all kinds of situations, and in some respects it may be a more effective outcome than we could have dreamed up, I don't know.

Frick: Are you primarily, then, dealing at the high school level?

Rogers: Well, the high schools and the college and we're really limited very much to that.

☼   ☼   ☼   ☼   ☼

Frick: One or two final questions, Dr. Rogers. You've been very kind this morning and I appreciate it very much. In my interview with Dr. Maslow, he stressed that the closer and closer he got to the end of his career, the more he has eliminated things from his life except almost a compulsive devotion to his theoretical studies and his writing. For example, he said that he recently cut out bird watching which was one of his favorite hobbies. He doesn't go to the theatre anymore with his wife. In other words, he has become almost totally dedicated to his professional work. And you know, when he was telling me this, he got very sad, and I felt that the tears were very near the surface. But this is a very committed man, obviously. Now, I thought I would like to have you tell me something about your life, Dr. Rogers. Is it as compulsively dedicated to your professional pursuits?

Rogers: Well let me . . . I *will* answer that. First of all, I would say that is the saddest thing about Abe Maslow that I've heard in a long time.

Frick: Did you know this?

Rogers: No. I sort of sensed that was the direction he was taking, but, God, to think of limiting one's life in that way! I really think that's a great mistake, because I don't believe that the best thinking comes from just shutting oneself away from a lot of outside stimulation.

Frick: You know, this is what I asked him. I asked him if this was self-actualizing and he wasn't too sure about this but, on the other hand, he said he was doing what was most vital and most crucial to him as an individual and he said he thought *that* was healthy. And he went on to say that there were times when, although he didn't go on bird walks anymore, he tried to be by himself. I asked Dr. Maslow, then, if these other interests and activities didn't feed back into his work. I mean, going to see a play, or . . .

Rogers: . . . or watching the birds.

Frick: That's right and I guess I have wondered, Dr. Rogers, if this was the direction you were taking.

Rogers: My direction is almost directly the opposite. I feel that . . . I've tried to face the reality of the fact that I hope I will continue to make some contributions, but I do feel that my most creative years are past. I hope that maybe some wisdom accrues as one grows older. For that reason, I'm not eager to turn out lots more writings. I do still continue to write quite a good deal, but certainly not compulsively, and I am the same as I always have been, in that I get my nourishment from direct contact with what I'm thinking about. That's why it isn't accidental at all that I would conduct a giggling group of high school girls for a whole weekend, and profit enormously. And I understand my granddaughters better on account of that.

Frick: Yes, they're about that age now, aren't they?

Rogers: Yes, we have an awfully good relationship with our oldest granddaughter, it just pleases me deeply that she will talk with us and particularly talk with me about things that are very, very crucial and delicate and personal. When I think what I would have told my grandparents, which would have been zero, then it just seems incredible to me. It seems as though a real change in culture *has* taken place when . . .

Frick: You're really bridging a gap, aren't you there, and you feel it.

Rogers: Yes. Jack Butler at Chicago once told me, when I said I was going to Wisconsin, partly because I felt that I had done what I could at the University of Chicago Counseling Center, and I wanted now to work more in a general department—well, at Wisconsin I was to have two departments to work in, psychiatry and psychology—and felt I didn't need to have a special group of my own. When I told Jack Butler this he said, "Why, you can never get along without a group of your own." Well, by and large, I guess he's proven to be right. I built a group there at Wisconsin and out here it's been the same thing, and I find enormous stimulation in always being with younger people. We have very few friends our own age. They're all younger people, and I get a lot out of that. For example, we have 40 people connected with the Center for Studies of the Person, a lot of them not on salary, and we always have various crazy kinds of informal associations, but I feel that I have an impact on that group. That's just as important as writing something. It's very exciting to me to see people go beyond what I can do and this would be one thing, I think, that Abe would be cutting himself off from. For example, in the business of being a person to another person in a therapy relationship, in a group situation or whatnot, I feel I've made a good deal of progress personally along that line. But then when I see the people who have worked with me, and who have gotten the stimulus for this from me, and are able to do it much more adequately, much more deeply than I can, I think that's *great*. I get a big kick out of that. And then, too, I guess another . . . well, I'll stick to myself and not Abe. . . . I build bird feeders in front of the house, and learn a great deal from watching the hummingbirds at their feeders. I don't think I would have nearly the belief in territoriality that I do, if I hadn't seen it operate under my nose. And I spend more time raising tuberous begonias than I ever would have spent at any previous portion of my life. I feel that . . .

Frick: . . . these are enriching now, especially at this time in your life.

Rogers: Yes. I feel . . . oh, for example, one change is that in the Center for Studies of the Person which is skating along on very thin, almost non-existent financial resources . . . in previous years, I would have felt very responsible for that group, because, like it or not, I'm sort of the ideological head of the place, even though I am not the administrator. This time I really comfortably do *not* feel that responsibility. I feel that these are mature young people, and that they know what they're getting into, and if the whole thing fails, they will all land on their feet, so I can relax and enjoy them and feel this is a damned good experience while it lasts. If it doesn't last very long, and if we do come a cropper financially, why, all right, it will have been a good experience. So, I guess I am much less compulsive about my work. I've turned down many opportunities for talks, and all that kind of thing.

Frick: You have to, don't you?

Rogers: Oh yes, I don't suppose I accept one in twenty and even that's too many. And I still like to keep having experiences at the grass roots level of human interaction. If I do contribute anything else theoretically it will be because of that and I will always be someone who is very much rooted in the earth of experience.

Frick: Your directions now, Dr. Rogers, are primarily in education, aren't they, or am I wrong now?

Rogers: I would say that the things I am involved in most deeply at the present time are, first of all, the intensive group experience with all different kinds of groups, encouraging other groups, and encouraging people to carry on groups that I haven't had much experience in, such as family groups and couples groups and adolescent groups. Then, certainly, that interest joins with an interest in education in this project we're carrying on to try to change an educational system. Then I have felt with increasing strength that I have quite a lot to say that is relevant to education, and have said it in a variety of different places, but most of it has been in the context of psychotherapy so that educators as a whole are not very familiar . . . or students in education are not very much aware of my point of view. And that's what's led me to work on this new book *Freedom to Learn*. And the third—these things keep changing in order of precedence from time to time—but third would be this interest which I don't feel very competent to follow, but I feel it's such a tremendously important question: What should be the philosophy of the behavioral sciences or what should the science of man really be? It should *not* be what it is at the present time, that I feel very sure of, but just what the answer is I don't know.

Frick: Dr. Rogers, in concluding our conversation this morning could you tell me a little bit more about your new adventure—or venture—probably both would be true, with the Center for Studies of the Person?

Rogers: Well. The Center for Studies of the Person is a very loosely organized group which could almost be called a non-organization. Yet, in spite of its lack of organizational structure, it has a tremendous sense of community and closeness. We are bound together by a number of common goals which I think could be summed up by saying that we are all interested in making it possible for man to enrich his own life and to expand his visions for himself. Thus, every summer some of our staff conduct a very large program for the training of facilitators of encounter groups because we feel that these have had a very enriching experience. Another large project coming to a conclusion is the attempt to make it possible for a whole complex educational system to bring about self-directed and forward-looking change in itself, thus making education more personal and more relevant. We also have a half dozen other projects going on at any given time. There are about 45 people who are members of the Center, 24 of them have their doctor's degrees.

I think we are also involved in something which we did not plan but which has gradually emerged. We are probably a pilot study in what the organization of the future might be, one that would really attract the loyalty and creativity of younger people. Our whole organizational purpose is to let each member do his own thing. He can freely join a project or a group and invest as much of himself in it as he wishes. The organization does not promise to support anyone but we help everyone as much as possible to find means of support. There is no one who is really in authority over any one else. Problems are settled through open discussion of feelings, attitudes, and facts. I am sure we have just as many problems as an hierarchical organization but they are a different quality of problem and the loyalty and enthusiasm and creativity of our staff is very, very high indeed. I think we represent the kind of organizational home that the person of tomorrow really desires.

Frick: Dr. Rogers, thank you very much.

Rogers: Well, it's been pleasant to talk with you.

part III

It has been stressed that the central focus, value, and impact of this book are the three interviews. However, as these interviews have unfolded, they have clearly illustrated that a personal commitment to a humanistic orientation, if it represents a unified and consistent philosophy, ecompasses and unifies practically all aspects of life.

My purpose in the following section is to provide a philosophical and theoretical context within which many of the facets of our conversations may be better understood, interpreted, and hopefully, more fully appreciated.

It has already been emphasized that humanistic psychology represents a general philosophical position regarding the nature of man, and encompasses a broad spectrum of theory, research, and applied studies. It is not surprising, therefore, that no specific theoretical system or position has emerged that is considered to provide a definitive statement of humanistic psychology. Many psychologists of different persuasions, though with varying degrees of involvement, are attracted to the humanistic movement in psychology because of its general orientation and the values which identify its image of man. If we *are* to identify a body of personality theory, however, that is most compatible and in greatest harmony with the humanistic orientation in psychology and the third force revolution, I believe we would discover that *holistic personality theory* would be a highly appropriate choice. In order to provide a theoretical context for the interviews and a unifying framework for further reflection upon them, Part 3 will present a holistic model of personality and some of its most important concepts and principles.[1] Holistic theory stresses that each dimension of personality, each facet, each identifiable part-function has a role in the development and functioning of the total organism. Each part-function and sub-system, however, must be viewed primarily in its relationship to a larger, more unified organization and purpose. Holistic personality theory endeavors to put man together again and make him whole. Its basic approach to personality study seeks to disclose those intrinsic features, inner dynamics, and system principles that contribute to man's total functioning and well being; to the actualization of his most noble, most creative potentials. Through this relatively recent approach to personality theory and research, we are discovering that there is an organic unity and wholeness in the growth of the human personality and a biological integrity that, if respected, nurtured, and encouraged to unfold and assert itself, has the power to transcend the more external and superficial determinants of personality development.

In the following chapters, I will endeavor to introduce the reader to a humanistic-holistic theoretical approach to the human personality and its development. The reader will quickly appreciate the fact that much of the interaction and material in the interviews evolved out of a shared interest in humanistic psychology and the orientation represented by holistic personality theory.

Chapter 4 presents a brief historical perspective on the development of the holistic approach to personality study. Chapter 5 is devoted to a statement and discussion of three major holistic principles or themes found in the writings of the three personality theorists to whom the reader has had a more personal introduction in

---

[1] This brief introduction to holistic personality theory should be considered a preface to a more fully developed statement and interpretation which is now in preparation by the author.

the interviews. The three major holistic themes to be discussed in Chapter 5 are: (1) *Organization:* The personality as an organized, dynamic and open system in which there is a striving for perfect order and symmetry. (2) *Motivation:* The development of the human personality unfolds out of one sovereign need or drive. (3) *Process:* The growth of the personality is directional and always evolving in a process of change toward a never-to-be reached unity and fulfillment.

In the final chapter I present a fourth basic theme of holistic personality theory, and one that is also stressed in the writings of Maslow, Murphy, and Rogers. This theme is *potentiality*. It is developed by presenting three theories of healthy personality as interpreted from the writings of our three personality theorists. Any theory of positive mental health or healthy personality must rest in large measure upon our image of man and our perception of his nature and potentials. We are, in each case, working with an ideal image or, as Gordon Allport has phrased it, with "theoretical man." In Chapter 6, therefore, we present three views of man in terms of his possibilities and potentials; three theories of "theoretical man."

4

Historical Perspective on
Holistic Personality Theory

The precursors of the articulated point of view that we find in the holistic personality theorists did not belong to a single "movement" or school of thought and we find that they did not share, nor do we, the advantages and disadvantages of a monolithic philosophical or theoretical stream as do the neo-Freudians and neo- or quasi-behaviorists. When we examine the various contributions to the philosophical and theoretical development of holistic thought we do not encounter any linear conceptual progression. At first glance they each seem isolated, scattered, and fragmentary and in an ironic sense, curiously unholistic. However, the variety of conceptual schemes available to us for the interpretation of reality is limited (4) and we discover that compatible and corresponding schemes do appear in fields as seemingly diverse as neurology and biology, (14, 19, 21, 6,) philosophy (22, 18, 8) and psychosomatic medicine (9). Seminal contributions to the fashioning of contemporary holistic or organismic theory have also come from the psychobiology of Adolf Meyer (17), from Bertalanffy's work in system theory (5, 4) and from the Gestalt movement in psychology initiated by Wertheimer, Koffka, and Kohler and in its later, more specific applications to personality theory by Lewin (15). Thus, the wide applicability of a holistic orientation can be seen by the range of fields, the diverse scientific disciplines and points of view represented here.

The following sections of this chapter will be concerned with a brief discussion of the contributions of the following men: Jan C. Smuts, John Hughlings Jackson, G. E. Coghill, John Dewey, Alfred North Whitehead, L. Von Bertalanffy, Adolf Meyer, and Kurt Lewin.

JAN. C. SMUTS

The title of Patron Saint of holistic theory, as it has evolved, must be awarded to the great scholar-soldier-statesman Jan Christian Smuts, for many years the Prime Minister of Africa and one of the key architects of the League of Nations. Smuts' personality and his creative and dramatic style of life reminds us of Churchill, and his concepts of the holistic character and evolution of life and the universe certainly achieves its most powerful validity and expression in the growth of his own personality. It is clear that Smuts, as few men do, lived his philosophy.

As a biologist and philosopher he was an amateur and yet, with his publication of *Holism and Evolution* in 1926 came one of Smuts' greatest personal achievements and, in retrospect, perhaps his most seminal contribution. Sinnot (20) in an introduction to a recent edition of Smuts' work, credits this amateur status as being partially responsible for the freshness and originality of his insights and concepts. That is, Smuts was able to develop his ideas ". . . with no preconceptions, no confirmed habits of thought, and no commitment to a scientific orthodoxy . . ." [1]

Smuts was not only a highly original thinker but genuinely prophetic, and many of the holistic personality theorists, each in his own idiom, reflect his views with surprisingly little alteration. Working his way on the debatable borderland between science and philosophy, Smuts developed his thesis of holism around such concepts as space, time, and matter, the cell, mechanism, evolution, and finally, the development of the personality. Ansbacher (3) considers Smuts to be the primary inspiration of the entire holistic movement and Ansbacher judges the early controversy between the deterministic, mechanistic point of view and that of holism and organicism that Smuts discussed over forty years ago to be a continuing and vital issue today. Smuts considered every facet of life as an integral part of a synthetic tendency in the universe and engaged in an evolutionary pilgrimage toward the development and articulation of greater unity and the creation of larger and more highly integrated wholes.

Smuts is not only an important exponent of a general holistic theory of evolution and the universe, but he is also of considerable interest to us in his application of these holistic concepts to personality. Smuts, even in his undergraduate days at Cambridge, was in-

---

[1] Edmund W. Sinnot, "Introduction to the Compass Edition," in *Holism and Evolution*, by J. C. Smuts. (New York: The Viking Press, Inc., 1961), p. ix.

rested in personality development and he wrote a paper, "Walt
Whitman: A Study in the Evolution of Personality." This undergraduate study clearly adumbrated his later interest in personality
and its holistic evolution. A subsequent paper, "An Inquiry into the
Whole," written as early as 1910, reflected a wider and more sophisticated application of the holistic principles he had first perceived in the personality development of Whitman. "Gradually, I
came to realize that personality was only a special case of a much
more universal phenomenon, namely, the existence of wholes and
the tendency toward wholes and wholeness in nature." [2]

For Smuts, however, the highest form of holistic integration to
be found in all of nature and the culmination of the long process of
progressive creation is to be found in the development of personality. Personality, according to Smuts, is ". . . the culminating phase
of the great holistic movement in the universe . . . Personality is the
supreme embodiment of Holism both in its individual and its universal tendencies. It is the final synthesis . . ." [3]

Mind, for Smuts, is the most important and conspicuous con-
stituent of personality and is endowed with consciousness. With
mind and consciousness comes purpose which is ". . . probably the
highest, most complex manifestation of the free, creative, holistic
activity of the mind." [4]

Considering the dedication and originality in his writings it is
not hard to believe, as Hall and Lindzey (10) suggest, that Smuts'
book was very influential. However, it is difficult to appraise his direct influence on the holistic personality theorists. In spite of the
fact that Smuts coined the word *holism* from the Greek word *holos*,
meaning complete or whole, and applied the concept to the development of the personality, we seldom find reference to his name.

JOHN HUGHLINGS JACKSON

Some strong roots of holistic theory must also be traced to the
work of the brilliant English neurologist-philosopher Hughlings
Jackson (14) and to his concepts of the evolutionary development of

---

[2] Jan C. Smuts, *Holism and Evolution* (New York: The Viking Press, Inc., 1961), Preface, vi.
[3] Ibid., p. 261ff.
[4] Ibid., p. 259.

the central nervous system and the hierarchical levels of this deve
opment. His concept of the evolutionary process of the central ne
vous system is essentially an integrative and holistic one and
based on a multilevel analysis of the nervous system. He saw th
process as going from highly organized lower centers of the syste
to higher, less well-organized ones; from simple to complex center
and from relatively automatic, mechanical centers to more aut
nomous, voluntary ones. Such an evolutionary process of human d
velopment proceeds, according to Mazurkiewicz, a chief inte
preter of Jackson's work, by superimposing new dynamics on o
ones, but not destroying them (7).[5] Jackson's philosophical-i
tegrative theories of neurological development have, for mar
years, served as one major frame of reference in the interpretatic
of psychological, psychopathological, and neurological phenomen

G. E. COGHILL

As with Smuts, the adumbration of Coghill's later personal ar
professional contributions took place at the collegiate level and r
flected an early interest in the nature and possible integration
sensation, perception, and thought. Early in his career, Coghill r
jected the traditional neuroanatomy of the day that dealt with di
crete elements that led, ultimately, to a mechanistic "switchboarc
concept of the human nervous system.

With the *Amblystoma* as primary subject, Coghill sought holi
tic reference points that would link behavior and neurological d
velopment. His search for such reference points centered arou
the answer to the question: Does behavior develop in an orderl
predictable manner? Coghill (6) proceeded, in well-executed r
search studies on the locomotion development patterns of *Ambly*
toma, to establish neurological correlates with sequential behavi
and development. Three major conclusions, now classic in their si
nificance, followed Coghill's studies (6).

1. Behavior patterns develop in a sequential order which para
    lels the order of development of the nervous system and i
    parts.

---

[5] See also the introduction to Dabrowski's work by Jason Aronson.

2. Physiological processes follow the order of their prior embryological development in the functions of aquatic and terrestrial locomotion and feeding.
3. Behavior develops, from the beginning, through the progressive expansion of a perfectly integrated total pattern and the individuation within it of partial patterns which acquire various degrees of discreteness.

Coghill's work enabled him to see the growth of the neuron and actual behavior of the organism in close relation to each other under controlled conditions. He showed that the form and pattern of behavior in *Amblystoma* paralleled the step-by-step order of growth in particular parts of the nervous system. This interaction and its concomitants led Coghill to reject the neuron theory as ". . . a fixed unit of structure and function." [6] Hooker's studies at Pittsburgh confirmed the application of Coghill's principles by applying them to the development of early overt behavior in the human infant (12,13).

From Coghill's work, two simultaneous processes emerged: (1) the growth expansion of the total pattern of the organism as an integrated unit, and (2) the development of specificity or individuation, emerging as "figure on ground" out of the prior integration. These finer processes of individuation emerge ". . . as a special feature within a more diffuse but dominant mechanism of integration of the whole organism." [7] Referring again to the neuron theory, Coghill (6) concludes that these two complex processes cannot be regarded as the simple action of chains of neurons without some welding into the organism as a whole.

From the beginnings of life, Coghill concludes, there is conclusive evidence of a pervasive organic unity and the basic function of the nervous system is to maintain the integrity of the individual as a whole while the individual is growing and creating himself. "Man is more than the sum of his reflexes, instincts, and immediate reactions of all sorts. He is all these plus his creative potential for the future." [8]

---

[6] G. E. Coghill, *Anatomy and the Problem of Behavior* (London: Cambridge University Press, 1929), p. 81.
[7] *Ibid.*, p. 89.
[8] *Ibid.*, p. 109.

Commenting on Coghill's work, Herrick (11), a former teacher and colleague, remarks that the partial-patterns—the discrete specializations—are concerned with analysis of experience and resulting action while the holistic total-patterns are synthetic or integrative and maintain the integrity of the organism in the interests of total development and functioning.

In summary, Coghill states:

> All reflexes emerge as partial or local patterns within an expanding or growing total pattern that normally is from the beginning perfectly integrated . . . they are inherently components of the total pattern or they are under its dominance. An instinctive reaction, on the other hand, is the total pattern overtly in action . . . the mechanism of the total behavior pattern is, therefore, the agency of integration.[9]

ADOLF MEYER

Dr. Adolf Meyer, one of the most influential figures in American psychiatry is credited by Whitehorn and Zilboorg (23) with initiating in American psychiatry the tradition of respect for the whole character of an individual's life. Dr. Meyer's emphasis on this totality implied a new and deeper individualization of therapeutic effort. Meyer, through his psychobiological approach, presented a more comprehensive union of conflicting theories.

Meyer did not believe that it was necessary to dissect the person into detachable elements in order to be scientific. He rejected Cartesian dualism and emphasized in his psychobiological approach that the primary unit of integration was the whole person.

> If mind were split from body, neither could exist and operate by itself, but their union in a person obviously provides quite a different state. of experience, without having to be broken down by preliminary analysis. Such integral units have their specific organization which is more than the mere summation of their component parts.[10]

For Meyer the study of an isolated part-function becomes recognizable as a part of the total person as soon as memory and con-

---

[9] G. E. Coghill, "The Genetic Interrelation of Instinctive Behavior and Reflexes," *Psychological Review* 37 (1930): 264–266, 264ff.

[10] Adolf Meyer, *The Common Sense Psychiatry of Dr. Adolf Meyer*, ed. A. Liet (New York: McGraw-Hill, 1948), p. 559. Quotation from address delivered by Dr. Meyer at the Henry Phipps Psychiatric Clinic: Fiftieth Anniversary Celebration, The Johns Hopkins Hospital 1939.

iousness are allowed to enter in, thus becoming a true psy-
obiological functioning.

In his psychobiological point of view Dr. Meyer made an expli-
t distinction between the functioning of detachable organs and
e role these same organs play in the "he" or "she" or in the "you"
d "I." He was certainly echoing the words of John Dewey when
made a distinction between the knee-jerk when the slightly
retched tendon is hit and the anticipatory action of the whole per-
n in this phenomenon. This common orientation may explain the
ct that Meyer looked upon Dewey as the greatest exponent of
merican philosophical thought (17).

In his long and active career Dr. Meyer was frequently at odds
ith the prevailing assumptions of behaviorism and psychoanalysis.
e decried the fragmented and compartmentalizingapproach of
ychoanalysis and its narrow conception of man built around sex-
l pathology. Meyer could only conceive of man's mind, behavior,
d organs as a biological whole and was most critical of behav-
rism in its evasion or denial of the subjective in man and its con-
sion over the mental aspects.

At seventy-five years of age, following his resignation from the
hns Hopkins University in 1941, Dr. Adolf Meyer continued to
eak out against the rigidity of scientific dogma, and to bring the
hole person into exclusive focus, the major foundation of his psy-
obiology.

FRED NORTH WHITEHEAD

Alfred North Whitehead, in his writings and lectures, con-
tently maintained a holistic posture regarding his concepts of be-
vior, world, and the unity of the universe. Atomistic, fact-bound
ought is the apex of abstractive intelligence and yet: "A single
ct in isolation is the primary myth required for finite thought, that
to say, for thought unable to embrace totality." [11]

Whitehead believed that connectedness is of the essence of all
ings and when this connectedness character of types and events is
st there has been an omission of essential factors in the fact con-
ered. Such a focus on "matter-of-fact" makes learning "a fugi-

---

[11] Alfred N. Whitehead, *Modes of Thought* (New York: G. P. Putnam's Sons, 1958), p. 12.

tive, and a cloistered virtue" [12] that avoids the essential relatio
ships that reveal the universe and its influence upon individual e
perience.

Whitehead spoke out on the need for integration and he soug
to resolve the mind-body-environment dichotomies. He maintaine
that mind and body were a complex unity and, in addition, th
there was no way to identify or define a demarcation between bo
and external nature. Where does the body become separate and d
tinct from environment and when does environment cease to be
part of the body, Whitehead asked. We find the holistic personali
theorists echoing the same questions and the same concern.

Whitehead pleaded for a concept of experience that is evolve
and structured out of an intimate relationship to the rest of thing
a concept of the evolving of experience so that new relationshi
are formed to create new and more highly evolved centers of unit
"The present receives the past and builds the future." [13] Whitehe
saw such modes of unity in the organization of molecules, ston
and in the lives of animals and men. However, he stressed that t
universe can never bend to complete stability and points out t
virtues of the frustration of order. Whitehead suggests a concept
disintegration as a stimulus for growth wherein there develops ne
and dominant forms of unity and order.

> The essence of life is to be found in the frustrations of established order.
> The universe refuses the deadening influence of complete conformity. [14]

For Whitehead, process and individuality require each oth
They are interdependent with process serving as the matrix or co
text within which individuality finds expression. In harmony wi
Smuts, Whitehead's vision was centered on the ever-evolving a
dynamic wholes amid diversity. It is this process that bestows i
pact upon the future as potentialities evolve and are actualized.

The idea of "static actuality" was anathema to Whitehead as
precluded the concept of potentiality. Whitehead stressed the "t
coming" nature of man, his process character, his future orie
tation, and his intentionality.

---

[12] *Ibid.*, p. 27.
[13] *Ibid.*, p. 43.
[14] *Ibid.*, p. 119.

The laws of life and nature, according to Whitehead, cannot be
en as static structures and as discrete entities. Every abstraction
evitably neglects significant factors which are inexorably related
 the wider patterns. A limited universe is thus created by a spe-
ial science. Attention to this theme is evident in the writings of the
olistic personality theorists and especially parallels Angyal's con-
ept of "parenthetic exclusions" where the organism and environ-
ent are viewed by the sciences as static structures separable in
ace. Aspects of the biospheric total field are thus abstracted and
udied by the various segmental sciences (2).

Whitehead believed, above all, in the essential unity and pat-
rn character of the human person and the engagement of this
nity to a future ideal and to the process of self-creation. In this
rocess Whitehead saw a certain time-binding integration of the
ast-present-future.

)HN DEWEY

John Dewey was one of the first to criticize the atomistic focus
 psychology and his specific target in his epoch-making article
as the stimulus-response model and the reflex arc concept, so
haracteristic of the psychology of his day. Dewey (8) considered
e reflex arc concept to be a survival of Plato's metaphysical dual-
m and, similarly, he criticized the tacit assumption in the reflex-
rc theory that the outcome of the resulting response is a totally
ew experience. Thus, Dewey saw the reflex-arc concept as ". . . a
atchwork of disjointed parts . . ." [15] He stressed the need in psy-
hology for a unifying principle and for a central and integrating
orking hypothesis. "The material is too great in mass and too var-
d in style to fit into existing pigeon-holes . . ." [16]

. VON BERTALANFFY

Underlying all of the above humanistic-holistic orientations we
e man viewed as a dynamic and open system in free exchange
ith the environment in contrast to a closed system subject to en-
ophy, loss of energy, and where there is little or no transaction

---

[15] John Dewey, "The Reflex-Arc Concept in Psychology," *Psychological Review*, 3 (1896):
57–370.
[16] *Ibid.*, p. 357.

with the environment. Bertalanffy has long advocated a concept of
the organism as an open system (4,5). He introduced the concept of
"equa-finality" to suggest that the final state of an organism is no
necessarily determined by initial conditions as seen in most close
physical systems. Here, we may define a system as a complex of ele
ments in mutual interaction as contrasted to simple reaction theo
ries and mechanistic determinism. For Bertalanffy, the human o
ganism represents a complex open system, active as well a
reactive, and engaged in a creative and uniquely human process.

> "Goal seeking behavior is a general biological characteristic; true pur-
> posiveness is a privilege of man and is based upon the anticipation of
> the future in symbols. Instead of being a product, man becomes the cre-
> ator of his environment." [17]

Allport (1), in a related article, builds upon Bertalanffy's contr
bution and specifically relates this concept of the open system t
personality theory. Allport stresses that while most contemporar
psychologists and personality theorists accept a semi-open syste
of the human organism, agreeing that there is an intake and outpu
of matter and energy and that the organism achieves and maintair
a steady state, few regard the organism as a completely open sy
tem. Allport indicates that most current semi-open system suppor
ers would object to at least two important criteria of the fully ope
system:

1. Such systems tend to enhance their degree of order and be
   come something more than they now are.
2. There is more in the truly open system than mere intake an
   output of matter and energy; there is extensive transaction
   commerce with the environment.

KURT LEWIN

It is in viewing human functioning via these system principle
that Gestalt psychology was nurtured in protest. The Gestalt psy
chologists were characterized by their opposition to "atomism." I
part, at least, the early development of the Gestalt movement was
reactionary one in opposition to both structural psychology, wit

---

[17] L. Von Bertalanffy, "Theoretical Models in Biology and Psychology," in *Theoretic
Models and Personality Theory*, eds. David Krech and George S. Klein (Durham: Duke Un
versity Press, 1952), p. 37.

its mental analysis into elements, and behaviorism. Thus, organization, relatedness, and pattern were major themes stressed by the Gestaltists. In concept and philosophy, therefore, Gestalt psychology has certainly m de an impact on the development of holistic personality theory as well as upon the larger arena of modern psychological thought. Although the former influence has been considerable and the two areas are warmly compatible, it must be pointed out that Gestalt psychology cannot be regarded as a truly holistic or organismic psychology. Historically, its attention has been directed primarily to sensory phenomena and the phenomenon of conscious awareness and, as developed by Wertheimer, Koffka, and Kohler, has not addressed itself to personality organization and personality development as a whole. Maslow, too, points out th t the Gestalt psychologists have limited their work primarily to the organization of the phenomenal world and to the various "fields" outside the organism (16). Holistic theory, then, may be seen as the extension and amplification of many of the Gestalt principles as applied to personality theory and to the organism as a whole.

The psychologist most responsible for utilizing Gestalt principles and concepts and employing them to advantage in understanding the personality and the totality of the organism was the brilliant psychologist and exponent of field theory, Kurt Lewin. Lewin, too, was reacting to the partitive concepts and reductionistic efforts seen in the stimulus-response behaviorism of his day, and he expressed a debt of gratitude for his background in Gestalt theory and to its major proponents Wertheimer and Kohler. He was closely associated with both men and it is clear that Gestalt theory served as a major foundation for Lewin's singular contributions to personality theory. Lewin's field theory, however, proved much more psychological in nature and constrasted, somewhat, with the physicalistic emphasis of Gestalt psychology.

Lewin stressed the unity of mind and made a protest against the piecemeal dissection of the mind into discrete elements, sensations, and feelings. However, according to Lewin, we cannot contend that everything is related to everything else. In judging the importance of a single experience or event it must be evaluated in terms of its embedded position in "spheres of the personality and whole processes." [18] One event may be linked to one system or process and another contiguous experience may be bound primarily within another system or sub-system. Thus, for Lewin, ordered action depends upon some partial segregation of systems.

Lewin, in a rejection of "associationism" and habit hierarchies, criticized the idea of discrete cause-effect relationships or "mechanically rigid" couplings in an effort to explain psychical events. He supported the idea, just beginning to gain some currency at the time of his writing, that we are not dealing with rigid connections of discrete elements but rather with "temporally extended wholes" [19] as in a melody.

Lewin emphasized the dynamic relationship between the person and his environment with such concepts as "life-space" and "field-forces" and, anticipating the holistic personality theorists, he insisted upon the contemporaneousness of all motivation. Lewin sought to transcend traditional dichotomies including the firmly established boundaries between person and world. To Lewin, the person and the environment meet one another in an organized, dynamic field. According to Murphy's interpretation

> "Kurt Lewin and other creative thinkers in the land of "field-theory" have undertaken to show that the "life space" of man is a function neither of man's inner existence nor of his environment nor of some bland formula regarding the interaction of the two, but of *new creations of possible systems of relationship between man and his environment*." [20]

In some respects Lewin failed to fully elaborate a psychology of the individual and in his later years he devoted himself almost entirely to a study of group processes, group dynamics, and action research (10). In contrast, holistic personality theory becomes, more completely than any other, a psychology of the organism or total person. It was Lewin, however, who was instrumental in developing a conceptual bridge between the Gestaltists and the holistic theorists. It was his theory that helped bring about a revival of man seen as a highly complex, creative energy system, behaving within a given field and motivated by psychological forces (10).

In some ways, of course, these diverse forerunners of holistic personality theory held little in common. In at least two important respects, however, they represent an important expression of con-

---

[18] Kurt Lewin, *A Dynamic Theory of Personality* (New York: McGraw-Hill, 1935), p. 54.
[19] *Ibid.*, p. 44.
[20] Gardner Murphy, *Human Potentialities* (New York: Basic Books, 1958), p. 21.

cern and commitment that advanced the evolution of holistic theory. First, they were all voicing a protest to the Cartesian mind-body dualism of the seventeenth century, to the American subscription to British Associationism in the nineteenth century, and to all other such attempts to abridge or compartmentalize the human organism. The second meeting of minds among these men of diverse interests and specialties is found in more than a negative and reactionary response to partitive concepts and the growing trend toward reductionism in the concepts and study of the human organism. Each man, in a manner appropriate to his own field of endeavor, sought to redress the imbalance and rectify, as he perceived it in his own profession, the violation to the essential nature and integrity of the organism which he firmly believed to be found in man's capacity for unity, organization, and integration. They all vigorously fought artificiality, over-simplification, and the unnecessary abridgment of human nature.

We have emphasized the fact that any theory of personality must ultimately rest, in large measure, upon our image of man and upon our perception of his nature and potentials. We are, in each case, working, as Allport prefers, with "theoretical man." We now present the holistic orientation to human life and growth. In this review the salient features of this orientation as applied to the human personality are presented in the following propositions.

Fifteen Propositions of a Holistic Theory of Personality

I.   The human organism possesses a distinct inner nature, an intrinsic nature of needs and directional tendencies. The holistic model for personality organization and growth is a biological one. There are inherent organismic directional tendencies that monitor and guide the development of the human personality. The organism must assert itself in these directions to insure healthy growth.

II. There is a natural impetus toward self-actualization; to enhance one's organism, one's life and development; to explore and enlarge upon one's potentials and capacities. Ergo, the human organism possesses both the capacity and desire for self-determination. In the course of growth the forging of a self-definition becomes a focal point of human striving.

III.   The concept of self-actualization includes both the need to establish unity and self-consistency as well as the urge for new stimulation leading to change, growth, and self-renewal.

IV.   The human organism's most basic strivings and directional tendencies are positive in nature. There is a distinctly social orientation to the character of human striving. Negative, destructive behaviors directed toward the self or toward others are the reactive consequences of frustration of needs closely associated with the basic directional tendencies.

V.   There is an organismic valuing process within the individual. This process evolves into a value system and becomes the integrating core of the personality.

VI.   These organismic species-wide value directions provide the base for universal criteria for healthy personality.

VII.   There is a discontinuity in human motivation. There is an emphasis upon the distinction between motivational life at low or arrested levels of human development and behavior and the motivational life of the healthy, mature adult. The difference might be likened to the motivational characteristics of the child as compared to that of a mature adult.

Holistic theorists reject the unconscious determinants and the reinforced behaviors of childhood as legitimate paradigms for mature, adult motivational life. In the former instance there is a psychopathological condition of average man that remains largely undetected.

VIII.   The human organism represents a dynamic time-Gestalt with heightened symbolic powers for integrating past, present, and future time in the interest of the whole personality.

IX.   Healthy personality always exists as future possibility. Unfinished structure, a sense of incompleteness, gives the organism impetus and a future-directed orientation.

X.   In healthy personality past experiences and future possibilities are of this moment, currently active in present time. Human motivation occupies a contemporaneous figure position within this time-Gestalt.

XI. The human organism and the environment are integral components comprising a larger sphere or field. There is reciprocity, an intimate mutuality of interaction within this field.

XII. The human organism maintains sovereignty within this dynamic organism-environmental field.

XIII. Human motivation, in its healthiest expression, is endowed with purpose and value: to actualize the distinctly human features of the organism and bring fruition to the highest development of one's capacities.

XIV. Healthy personality represents the emergence and successful articulation of the organismic, species-wide directional tendencies. These directional tendencies, while innate expressions of the organism, must receive nurture and support from the environment.

XV. Self-awareness is an essential component in the healthy growth of the organism. It is only through a deepening awareness that the individual can maximize his potentials, select his course, and enter into the process of his own growth.

❋   ❋   ❋   ❋   ❋

Four major themes appear to characterize holistic personality theory and command a large share of attention in the writings of the holistic theorists. These major themes delineate basic developmental principles that are crucial to holistic personality theory. They incorporate many of the propositions we have stated above.

Basic Holistic Themes

I. *Organization:* The human personality seeks to create a self-consistent organization, and bring some completion to incomplete structure. Personality is viewed as an organized whole and more than a mere aggregate of discrete parts. There is a desire for stability and a need to achieve unity and order.

II. *Process:* The personality is never a static, unchanging phenomenon. Rather, the personality is always in flux, evolving and in the process of undergoing change. There is movement toward higher levels of consciousness.

III.   *Sovereign Motivation:* The human organism is guided, energized and integrated by one sovereign need or motive; that of self realization.

IV.   *Potentiality:* Man has vast inner resources and unrealized potentials for growth. There is a major concern for the development of this human potential and for a conceptualization of healthy personality. There is a focus on normality and health rather than on psychopathology.

In the following chapter we will discuss the interpretation and treatment of the first three themes by our three theorists, Abraham Maslow, Gardner Murphy, and Carl Rogers. In chapter six, we will present theme four, *potentiality*, by developing each theorist's concepts of the healthy personality.

References

1. Allport, Gordon. "The Open System in Personality Theory." *Journal of Abnormal and Social Psychology* 61 (1960): 301–310.

2. Angyal, Andras. *Foundations for a Science of Personality.* New York: The Commonwealth Fund, 1941.

3. Ansbacher, H. L. "On the Origins of Holism." *Journal of Individual Psychology* 17 (1961): 142–144.

4. Bertalanffy, L. Von. Theoretical Models in Biology and Psychology. In *Theoretical Models and Personality Theory*, David Krech and George S. Klein, eds. Durham: Duke University Press, 1952.

5. Bertalanffy, L. Von. "The Theory of Open Systems in Physics and Biology." *Science* 3 (1950): 23–29.

6. Coghill, G. E. *Anatomy and the Problem of Behavior.* London: Cambridge University Press, 1929.

7. Dabrowski, Kazimierz. *Positive Disintegration.* Boston: Little, Brown and Co., 1964.

8. Dewey, John. "The Reflex Arc Concept in Psychology." *Psychological Review* 3 (1896): 357–370.

9. Dunbar, H. Flanders. *Emotion and Bodily Changes.* 4th ed. New York: Columbia University Press, 1954.

10. Hall, Calvin S. and Lindzey, Gardner. *Theories of Personality.* New York: John Wiley and Sons, Inc., 1957.

11. Herrick, C. Judson. *The Evolution of Human Nature,* Austin: University of Texas Press, 1956.

12. Hooker, Davenport. The Development of Behavior in the Human Fetus. In *Readings in Child Psychology*, Wayne Dennis, ed. Englewood Cliffs: Prentice Hall, Inc., 1951.

13. Hooker, Davenport. *The Origin of Behavior.* Ann Arbor: The University of Michigan, 1944.

14. Jackson, J. H. *Selected Writings of John Hughlings Jackson.* J. Taylor, London: Hodder and Stoughton, 1931.

15. Lewin, K. *A Dynamic Theory of Personality.* New York: McGraw-Hill, 1935.

16. Maslow, Abraham. *Motivation and Personality.* New York: Harper and Row, 1954.

17. Meyer, A. *The Common Sense Psychiatry of Dr. Adolf Meyer.* A. Liet, New York: McGraw-Hill, 1948.

18. Ryle, Gilbert. *The Concept of Mind.* London: Hutchinson & Co., Ltd., 1949.

19. Sherrington, C. S. *The Integrative Action of the Nervous System.* New York: Charles Scribner, 1906.

20. Sinnott, Edmund W. Introduction to the Compass Edition. In *Holism and Evolution,* Jan C. Smuts, ed. New York: The Viking Press, Inc., 1961.

21. Smuts, Jan C. *Holism and Evolution.* New York: MacMillan, 1926.

22. Whitehead, Alfred N. *Modes of Thought.* New York: G. P. Putnam's Sons, 1958.

23. Whitehorn, John C. and Zilboorg, Gregory. "Present Trends in American Psychiatric Research." *American Journal of Psychiatry* 13 (1933).

5

Basic Themes

ABRAHAM MASLOW

Organization: The personality is an organized, dynamic, and open system.

> ... The individual is an integrated and organized whole.[1] Isolated behavior tends to be on the fringe of life's main concerns. They are isolated simply *because* they are unimportant, i.e., have nothing to do with the main problems, the main answers, or the main goals of the organism.[2]

A persistent critic of scientific orthodoxy, Abraham Maslow (1,2) has relentlessly stressed the dangers inherent in a technique- and means-centered science where real problems, goals, and values are ignored in favor of techniques, methods, and apparatus. The consequence of means-centering is a timid, value-free science, unable to discriminate between the relevant and the inconsequential, peripheral problems and imposing arbitrary limits on its jurisdiction and responsibility. In the scientific study of personality this frequently means a refined technology geared toward highly reductive efforts to discover the convenient units that can be managed and manipulated by its sophisticated methodology. Science quickly becomes a closed and protective circle rather than engaged in an open and creative process of discovery in the realm of genuine and challenging problems and comprehensive human concerns.

Maslow (1) favors a problem-centered science that is less concerned with technology and reductive analysis and more committed to a holistic view that is both functional and dynamic. Maslow refers to this latter emphasis as the holistic-dynamic point of view. The holistic-dynamic point of view may be contrasted with

---

[1] Abraham Maslow, *Motivation and Personality.* (New York: Harper and Row, 1954), p. 63.

[2] *Ibid.*, p. 55.

the general-atomistic approach and its tendency to compartmentalize and oversimplify the basic units of personality and their
relationships. Maslow's holistic-dynamic emphasis suggests a syndrome concept of personality defined as, ". . . a structured, organized complex of apparently diverse specificities (behaviors,
thoughts, impulses to action, perception, etc.) which, however,
when studied carefully and validly are found to have a common unity . . ."[3] Each syndrome tends to be related and, behaviorally, an
expression of the whole, integrated personality.

The human organism, Maslow asserts, is not a collection of separate organs and functions. When we study a given act or behavior
it must be viewed as an expression of the whole organism rather
than as a discrete entity to suit the convenience of methodology.
There are no closed systems within the organism.

Motivation: The development of the human personality unfolds
out of one sovereign need, motive or drive.

> "The single holistic principle that binds together the multiplicity of hu-
> man motives is the tendency for a new and higher need to emerge as the
> lower need fulfills itself by being sufficiently gratified." [40]

As a preface to motivational theory, Maslow abandons the multiple drive concept of human motivation as theoretically unsound.
Such an atomistic listing of drives isolates one drive from the others, suggests a discreteness and mutual exclusiveness which does not
exist, and neglects their dynamic role in human behavior.

Consistent with other holistic theorists, Maslow (1,3) also rejects
a definition of motivation based on concepts of equilibrium, home-
ostasis, or drive reduction. According to Maslow, recent years of research and experience in psychotherapy, creativity, child psychology, and work with brain-injured soldiers have strongly
repudiated these theories. To supplant these inadequate and out-
moded concepts of human motivation Maslow posits an inherent
tendency to growth and self-perfection. We shall hereafter refer to
Maslow's sovereign motive as the *positive growth tendency.* This
term is considered to be free of the ambiguities found in the term

---

[3] Ibid., p. 32.
[4] Abraham Maslow, *Toward a Psychology of Being.* (Princeton: D. Van Nostrand Co.,
Inc., 1962,) p. 53.

self-actualization, since it encompasses the entire developmental "process-character" of motivation and therefore includes both the deficiency motives—strivings to meet the more basic needs—and the growth motives. Maslow defines growth as:

> ... the various processes which bring the person toward ultimate self-actualization ... Growth is seen, then, not only as progressive gratification of basic needs to the point where they "disappear," but also in the form of specific growth motivations over and above these basic needs, including talents, capacities, creative tendencies and constitutional potentialities.[5]

Maslow (1,3) conceives of human motivation as functioning along a hierarchy of instinctoid needs.[6] These needs, listed in order of prepotency, are: (1) the physiological needs, (2) the safety needs, (3) the belonging and love needs, (4) the esteem needs, (5) the need for self-actualization. The basic physiological needs must be satisfied before the organism can turn his attention to his safety needs. The safety needs, in turn, are prepotent over the organism's pursuit of his love needs. Thus, the gratification of each need in the hierarchy is a prerequisite for attention to the next.

While this hierarchy is ordered in a decreasing degree of instinctoid control, it represents, as the *positive growth tendency* gains momentum, an increasing degree of psychological health, movement toward full-humanness, and a qualitative change in the nature of the motivation (1). The progression is toward that ultimate value for mankind, self-actualization or toward ". . . becoming fully human, everything that the person *can* become." [7]

The needs below the level of self-actualization represent the deficiency motives and present the individual with the task of working through the problems and inevitable frustrations in achieving gratification within these basic need areas. At the level of self-actualization, however, the focus and quality of human motivation shifts from a deficiency motivated organism struggling to meet the dominant, prepotent needs in life, to an organism that is freed from lower-need bondage so that he can be concerned with satisfying the higher, though less dominant, needs.

---

[5] Ibid., p. 24.

[6] Maslow distinguishes between instincts and the instinctoid nature of basic needs. See Chapter 7, *Motivation and Personality*. Refer also to the interview with Abraham Maslow.

[7] Maslow, *Toward a Psychology of Being*, p. 145.

Process: The growth of personality is directional, always evolving, and undergoing change.

> The process of healthy growth is made up of a never ending series of free choice situations, at every point throughout life, in which he must choose between safety and growth.[8]

Maslow's need hierarchy emphasizes personality as process, directed by the *positive growth tendency* and evolving toward the ultimate values of the human organism. Following the existentialists, Maslow stresses the importance of the concept of future time in personality development where the present exists as potential and the future plays a dynamic role in its actualization. ". . . self-actualization is meaningless without reference to a currently active future." [9]

In a discussion of direction and process in personality development, it is important to point out that Maslow, in trying to capture the essence of the nature of self-actualization, distinguishes between the *process* of becoming and the pure states of "being" as found in the fleeting "peak" experiences and in other complete states of self-realization. In these latter "episodes" there seems to be almost a complete break with goal direction, struggling, striving. The needing, coping behavior and other characteristics so typically associated with the lower-level deficiency motives are absent. The more traditional motivation theories tend to lose their significance or relevance since motivational life appears to be different for self-actualizers. However, Maslow's concepts of the process of *becoming* a person and the achievement of the state of *being* a person are not altogether compatible and represent some minor theoretical problems.

If self-actualization represents the human being at the apex of his development in the form of integrated, non-striving states of "being," does the stage of self-actualization in human development also represent or imply a static state that marks the end of further growth and evolution of the personality? It is clear that Maslow acknowledges the conflict between a process-becoming psychology and an ultimate "being" psychology. "The danger with a pure Being-psychology," states Maslow, "is that it may tend to be static,

---

[8] Ibid., p. 45.
[9] Ibid., p. 14.

not accounting for the facts of movement, direction, and growth." [10] In another statement Maslow (3) suggests that self-actualization may be both an end goal and a penultimate stage in the process to reach the ultimate in self-transcendence, i.e., ego-transcendence and the loss of self in the peak experiences. Maslow, at times, speaks of the states of "being" as static states of perfection, a pinnacle of human development that transcends process and growth throughout the life span, even if some stage or level of self-actualization is reached. He seeks to purge the term of its static connotations and redefines self-actualization to refer to a "spurt" in the coalescing of the person's powers and representing an intensely efficient and enjoyable episode in the life of the person. Maslow (3) also indicates that an experience in pure *being* can promote further *becoming* and he suggests that they may be aspects of the same process.

Finally, we must say that it would be extremely inconsistent for Maslow to conclude that *being* and *becoming* were mutually exclusive or contradictory and although he does, at times, express some confusion over their relationship we find no basis to assert that he supports such a conclusion. Rather, his position seems to be that human growth never ceases to be a process, an engagement with the future, as new directions are discovered, as new wholes emerge and as previously unknown facets of the self come into being. During the episodes of self-actualization, however, there are more frequent experiences of pure *being* that transcend, for rare, but intense moments, the life-long process character of human development.

GARDNER MURPHY

Organization: The personality is an organized, dynamic and open system.

> Unconscious dynamics . . . call our attention to conflict, disunity, but personality also achieves a kind of genuine unity or wholeness . . . From this point of view, traits are not individual parts, but aspects of a totality. Each trait has "membership character" (to use the language of Gestalt Psychology) which places it in a contextual system . . .[11]

---

[10] Ibid., p. 42.
[11] Gardner Murphy, *Personality: A Biosocial Approach to Origins and Structure* (New York: Harper and Brothers Publishers, 1947), p. 20.

Man has always imposed a primitive, internal organization upon the demands, vicissitudes and caprice of his environment. However, the achievement of a creative unity and wholeness, according to Murphy, is not gained easily or quickly. He conceives of personality as passing through three rather distinct developmental phases, a hierarchy of organization and development. This hierarchy includes: (1) an early and undifferentiated, global mass, (2) a period marked by the appearance of differentiation, as recognizable parts emerge, and (3) finally, there is the development of an organization of the differentiated parts "so as to constitute a system." [12]

Global, undifferentiated qualities would include motor, sensory and affective dispositions: metabolic rhythms, various thresholds of response, and all of the more primordial dispositions that characterize the organism (6). These global qualities, the ubiquitous dispositions, express themselves in every new response and transition. The differentiated parts of stage two reflect aspects of its global heritage. There is a "phenomenon of correspondence" existing between the original global dispositions and the characteristics of the differentiated parts as well as a formal relationship between the parts themselves since ". . . they are all traceable to the same global matrix." [13]

Finally, in stage three there is an emergence of *congruence,* an integration of the relatively discrete aspects of personality around goal-directed behavior. "Traits appearing at stage two when integrated with others at stage three have such membership character that they can no longer be understood at all outside their full personality contexts." [14] True "architectural wholeness" is demonstrated when the second and third level traits achieve interdependence.

With congruence, then, comes a unity and harmony revolving upon central values or goals that characterize the entire pattern of life. This complex and sophisticated system, the "architectural whole," while representing a synthesis, is not a closed and rigid structure. Murphy (6) stresses that it is in constant motion and retains the capacity for internal reorganization as well as free adaptation to new situations and circumstances.

---

[12] Ibid., p. 619.
[13] Ibid., p. 621.
[14] Ibid., p. 627.

Murphy's interpretation of the personality system and evolving holistic unity goes beyond the internal organization and processes of the organism and includes the possibility of more supreme integrations as man fashions new relationships with his environment. There is, in fact, no real distinction made between man and his environment and Murphy views man as ". . . a nodal region, an organized field within a larger field, a region of perpetual interaction, a reciprocity of outgoing and incoming energies." [15] So interlaced is man and his environment that man not only imposes structure upon his environment but the environment, through its function-controls, alters the structure of the organism (4). In this intimate reciprocity, the inner moves toward one with the outer. "It is a movement toward isomorphism." [16]

Motivation: The development of the human personality unfolds out of one sovereign need, motive, or drive.

> The term motivation . . . does not define a box that contains a few distinct tools for our use, but the abstraction of one of the properties of the living process—its stability, push, or as Bergson liked to call it, *élan*. Even if we could find where the push "starts" we should find other pushes cooperating . . . through a process of *fusion* rather than one of mechanical addition.[17]

While Gardner Murphy is a pronounced holistic theorist, he is also a thorough-going eclectic and his depth and breadth as a psychologist permits him an articulate, integrative view of the broad and sweeping domain of psychological knowledge and wisdom. Thus, as an eclectic, he is not a purist and does not take a dogmatic stance toward personality theory nor become a demanding proponent for a single point of view. We must refer to his works as representing an *integrative eclecticism.* In terms of motivation theory, therefore, Murphy's biosocial theory does not explicitly lend its conceptual support to a sovereign motive for human behavior. In fact, Murphy considers his entire work (6) to be concerned with motivation.

---

[15] Ibid., p. 7.
[16] Gardner Murphy and Herbert Spohn, *Encounter with Reality.* (Boston: Houghton Mifflin, 1968), p. 49.
[17] Murphy, *Personality: A Biosocial Approach, p. 89 ff.*

The basic motive structure, for Murphy, are the interacting tissue-tension systems within the organism. Thus, concentrations of energy promote tension-gradients—up or down—and become the motives of the organism. Murphy recognizes, therefore, that increasing tension in the form of anticipation, expectancy, and appetites can be as important to the motivation of the organism as tension reduction. He is critical of the atomistic, simplistic approaches to human motivation in the form of mechanistic theory and the emphasis in psychology on the tension reduction of visceral drives. Although Murphy recognizes tension reduction to be a primary force in infancy, he emphasizes that the conative goal of the organism is to keep activity going and to *maintain* the energy system. While he regards the infantile energy systems as "patterned bundles of motivation" [18] Murphy feels that they must undergo a long process to become the complicated motivational patterns found in the adult organism.

Murphy, on the other hand, does not support a theory of distinct and separate motives. In his holistic approach to motivation, the biological and the social contributions form one sphere, one large and encompassing motivational structure. Therefore, while strongly emphasizing the biochemical base for motive structure, including aesthetic needs, or the "aesthetic or cosmic cravings," [19] Murphy also stresses the marked effects that the behavioral world and the cultural world can have upon the biochemical system. Thus, motivation is set squarely within a larger context; in an interacting organism-environment field.

Murphy (7,5) has been critical of the goal of self-actualization as a sovereign motive of the organism. The human being, Murphy argues, has an infinite number of selves or natures to realize and there is never just one goal toward which the organism is aiming. "No single drive could ever preempt the orchestration of the total without leading us back to a simple catalogue of independent drives waiting each by itself to be fulfilled . . ." [20]

In summary, it may be said that, at times, Murphy seems to be in need of a more unifying motivational principle. He is repetitive

[18] Ibid., p. 86.
[19] Ibid., p. 107.
[20] Gardner Murphy, *Human Potentialities.* (New York: Basic Books, Inc., 1958), p. 321.

in his emphasis on a plurality of "motives," "natures" and "selves" that evolve from the basic tissue-tension centers of the organism and the integration of these motives within the organism is, for Murphy, a central theme. What then, we may ask, serves as the integrating force or factor and gives direction and meaning to the tension gradients and energies? Is there no unifying force that guides and integrates the direction of these human energies and characterizes the life process? The only hormic principle that Murphy explicitly acknowledges is the conative character of all activity.

Murphy has made substantial contributions to personality theory with his integrative eclecticism and his synoptic biosocial approach to the understanding of the human organism. It may be an unfortunate consequence of his eclecticism, however, that precludes his serious consideration of a unifying trend or motivational force in organismic growth.

Process: The growth of personality is directional, always evolving, and undergoing change.

> ... personality is revealed more through its cycles and trends than through its cross section, more through its continuities and discontinuities, through change in its tissues and in its outer world, than through any inventory of the traits of the moment, however subtle.[21]

Murphy emphasizes the importance of the time dimension to the theme of process. After surveying the life of William James he states the significance of "... the time dimension, the changing, growing, self renewing processes of personality evolution, of release of personality in a new way in each situation." [22] According to Murphy, man's symbolic powers are crucial to the process conception of personality. He is not bound to a past or to a dependence on the current, external stimulus but may attend to the abstract and envision and plan for the future.

Murphy postulates three basic human natures that emerge within the process of human development. His *first human nature* is the "raw" or "original" human nature. This original human nature is a direct product of evolution and reflects a general biochemical and nervous organization with the potential for individuality. Even at

[21] Murphy, *Personality: A Biosocial Approach*, p. 71.
[22] Ibid., p. 25.

this raw and primitive level, however, there are catalysts for process and change. Restless energy, curiosity, sensory hungers, and sensitivity are a part of the organism's undifferentiated biological core (5).

The emergence of culture, with its imprint of acquired tastes and traits, and uniform modes of living on the original human nature, represents the established domain of the *second human nature*. This protective shield of culture is seductively attractive to man and meets his needs for order, safety, companionship and co-operation. Behind this protective cover, however, man may undergo a process leading to rigidity, resistance to change and the standardization of the personality. In conflict with this set of social-protective needs are other, more profound attributes and needs of the original human nature that are not as readily satisfied. A given culture allows only a narrow range of the human potential to develop and flourish and man soon becomes frustrated over the uniformity of his habits and styles and the narrow scope of his existence. He is a restless seeker for his own uniqueness and individuality.

It is out of this frustration of certain important needs and potentials, Murphy suggests, that man actively pursues his quest for further fulfillment and is able to break through the firm mold of his culture. It is, in fact, this urge to discovery and a deeply embedded need to understand and encounter reality (4) that provokes man to step from his protective cultural shield and venture forth to meet his new requirements. It is this insistent urge to discover, explore, create and evolve that constitutes Murphy's *third human nature*.

It is the unfolding, elaboration, and integration of the three human natures that characterizes the process component of human development. It should be emphasized here that Murphy rejects the perfection of man as a viable concept or goal. The perfection of man has meaning to Murphy only if we conceive of a static universe or some end goal that precludes further process. ". . . he becomes qualitatively a new man as he grows; and there is no such thing as a society which will offer fulfillment to human nature. . . ." [23]

This evolutionary process, culminating in the third human nature and marked by quantitative and qualitative changes in both

---

[23] Murphy, *Human Potentialities*, p. 311.

man and society, does not imply a diminution and loss of the prior human natures. The crucial question is: How can all three natures be recognized, respected, and fulfilled? Murphy suggests that *"perhaps the three human natures, still in conflict with one another, can integrate in a new emergent whole."* [24]

If new combinations and integrations are to evolve and if the three human natures are to integrate in a new whole the *principle of emergence* will have to operate. The principle of emergence requires new conceptual tools as a base for the new forms of integration (5), in contrast to trial and error methods or poorly integrated changes that must conform to an outdated, existing structure. "Emergence defines the process by which co-working factors result in a *new form of organization."* [25] Ideally, these new forms of organization, as indicated before, are not exclusive within the organism but include a larger field that extends beyond the organism. ". . . human nature and society are evolving together not only along a line indicating quantitative increase in this or that but into ever new qualities." [26]

CARL ROGERS

Organization: The personality is an organized, dynamic, and open system.

> The most impressive fact about the individual human being seems to be his directional tendency toward wholeness . . .[27]

The holistic emphasis in Carl Rogers' theory of personality, as do all of his basic propositions, centers around the development of the concept of self, defined by Bischof in his interpretation of Rogers, as "being the strivings, emotional feeling, and ideas that the individual recognizes, interprets, and values as his very own." [28]

---

[24] Ibid., p. 252.

[25] Ibid., p. 258.

[26] Ibid., p. 311.

[27] Carl R. Rogers, "The Actualizing Tendency in Relation to 'Motives' and to Consciousness," in Nebraska Symposium on Motivation, vol. XI ed. Marshall R. Jones (Lincoln: University of Nebraska Press, 1963), p. 4.

[28] Ledford Bischof, *Interpreting Personality Theories* (New York: Harper and Row, 1964), p. 433.

The human infant quickly becomes the center of a phenomenological field, the guardian of a private world of experience. Gradually, this experienced and perceived field becomes "reality" for
the organism. The differentiated self, the perceived reality, gradually emerges out of a portion of this perceptual field. As the growing person encounters and interacts with his environment, perceives his reality, and as a self-concept comes into being and
evolves, there is, according to Rogers, a persistent effort on the part
of the organism to protect his "reality" and to achieve a unity and
wholeness of the self; a self-consistency (9,11).

Convincing evidence of Rogers' thesis concerning the self-consistent strivings of the personality was obtained in the observation
of clients undergoing psychotherapy. In the course of their therapy,
there were many erratic changes and shifting characteristics in the
personality as clients explored significant dimensions of the self and
struggled to reconstruct various aspects of their experience. Rogers'
observations indicated, however, that the product of their endeavors was clearly a Gestalt, in which the shifts and fluctuations of one
minor aspect could completely alter the entire pattern. The con-
figural nature of the self-concept seemed to be confirmed in these
studies.

One of the primary needs of the organism, then, is to maintain
an internal order and consistency of the self and achieve a state of
congruence; an accurate matching of experience and awareness.[29]
For optimum growth this not only demands a progressive revision
of the self-concept, based on an openness to experience, but an accurate symbolization and assimilation of these experiences in the
Gestalt of the self structure.

Additional propositions, taken from Rogers' (9) theory of personality and behavior, that extend the concept of integration and its
important role in the formation of the self-structure of the personality include:

> *XI. As experiences occur in the life of the individual, they are either*
> *a. symbolized, perceived and organized into some relationship to the self,*
> *b. ignored because there is no perceived relationship to the self-structure,*

---

[29] This term was first used by Rogers to describe a condition of openness to experience on
the part of the therapist and a matching of his genuine feelings with his behavior in relating
with the client. This accurate reflection of experience and awareness by the therapist is believed by Rogers to be one of the conditions facilitating growth in the client.

*c. denied symbolization or given a distorted symbolization because the
experience is inconsistent with the structure of the self. XII. Most of the
ways of behaving which are adopted by the organism are those which are
consistent with the concept of self. XVI. Any experience which is inconsistent with the organism or the structure of the self may be perceived as
a threat, and the more of these perceptions there are, the more rigidly the
self structure is organized to maintain itself.*[30]

One's interpretation of "science" and its appropriate role in the
study of man often reflects the image of man that prevails. Rogers'
view of the person as an essentially integrated being striving for increasing unity or "congruence" asks for a behavioral science that
will acknowledge and respect this attribute of wholeness. Rogers
(10,12) is critical of "modes of knowing" that are limited to a study
of the peripheral acts and external behaviors of man, while ignoring
the richly patterned and genuinely heuristic phenomonological
variables.

Motivation: The development of the human personality unfolds
out of one sovereign need, motive, or drive.

> ... I would reaffirm ... my belief that there is one central source of
> energy in the human organism; that it is a function of the whole organ-
> ism rather than of some portion of it; and that it is perhaps best con-
> ceptualized as a tendency toward fulfillment, toward actualization, to-
> ward maintenance and enhancement of the organism.[31]

Carl Rogers postulates an all-embracing motive, the actualizing
tendency to account for the full range of human behavior and development. It is a positive directional tendency underlying all behaviors including those expressions that seem to contradict such inherent positive strivings for self-enhancement. In these latter
instances, Rogers expresses the conviction that they are neurotic or
perverted expressions of the actualizing tendency growing out of a
state of incongruence, i.e., a discrepancy or dissociation between
the organism's experience and awareness. Such experiences have
been inaccurately symbolized thereby encouraging maladaptive or
self-defeating expressions of the basic actualizing tendency. Thus,

---

[30] Carl R. Rogers, *Client-Centered Therapy* (Boston: Houghton Mifflin Co., 1951), p. 503 ff.
[31] Carl R. Rogers, "The Actualizing Tendency in Relation to 'Motives' and to Con-
ciousness," in *Nebraska Symposium on Motivation*, ed. Marshall R. Jones (Lincoln: Univer-
ity of Nebraska Press, 1963), p. 6.

the matrix for all human motivation and behavior is the tendency toward growth, maintenance and enhancement of the organism.

Rogers (8) seriously questions the value and necessity of post ulating additional motivational constructs. He does not deny, of course, the existence of a variety of motives and drive states in the human organism but he feels that to pursue these discrete motives would distract from significant research and be of little heuristic value. The *actualizing tendency*, as the sovereign motive, encom passes all such discrete motives and drives and lends itself to the in terpretation of the organism as a complex being with a tendency to ward self-consistency or wholeness. Rogers believes that a great variety of motives and behaviors could be subsumed under the ac tualizing tendency but the tendency exerts itself largely in ". . . the actualization of that portion of the experience of the organism which is symbolized in the self." [32]

There are strong autonomous concomitants within Rogers' ac tualizing tendency. The trend is ". . . away from heteronomy, or control by external forces." [33] Philosophically, this discounts the de clining "empty organism" school of thought and places man at the helm to chart his own developmental course.

Process: The growth of personality is directional, always evolving and undergoing change.

> Life, at its best, is a flowing, changing process in which nothing is fixed . . . *it is always in process of becoming.* (italics mine) [34]

The natural trend of the organism is to engage itself in a di rectional process where "past and future are both in this mo ment . . ."[35] Organismic life moves in a direction characterized by flexibility and change and it is not a fixed system. It is a process of increasing wholeness and enhancement of the organism: a process of becoming.

---

[32] Carl R. Rogers, "Therapy, Personality and Interpersonal Relationships as Developed in the Client-Centered Framework," in *Psychology: A Study of a Science*, Vol. III. *Foundation of the Person in the Social Context*, ed. S. Koch (New York: McGraw-Hill, 1959), p. 196.

[33] Ibid.

[34] Carl R. Rogers, *On Becoming a Person* (Boston: Houghton Mifflin, 1961), p. 27.

[35] Carl R. Rogers, "Toward a Modern Approach to Values: The Valuing Process in the Mature Person," *Journal of Abnormal and Social Psychology* 6, No. 2 (1964): p. 164.

Rogers' research in psychotherapy and his concern and search for the substantive attributes of the helping relationship have served as the basic foundations for his self-theory of personality. The major theme of *process,* too, grew out of Rogers' intimate, first-hand experiences with clients in psychotherapy. He came to view his clients' experiences in psychotherapy as experiences characterized by process. Rogers observed that clients began this process of therapy ". . . from a point of fixity . . ." [36] but they soon became engaged in an emerging continuum characterized by a gradual loosening of feelings, an increase in the flow and openness of expression, a greater capacity for immediacy of experiencing and an increased clarity of communication both within and outside the therapeutic relationship. It was not this important process character of the clients' therapeutic experiences, per se, however, that was regarded as most significant. It was the fact that the clients did not move from their original point of fixity to another level of fixity. Instead, Rogers observed that his clients had become ". . . an integrated process of changingness." [37]

---

[36] Rogers, *On Becoming a Person,* p. 158.
[37] *Ibid.*

References

Maslow, Abraham.

1. *Motivation and Personality.* New York: Harper and Row, 1954.

2. *The Psychology of Science: A Reconnaissance.* New York: Harper and Row, 1966.

3. *Toward A Psychology of Being.* Princeton: D. Van Nostrand Co., Inc., 1962.

Murphy, Gardner.

4. (with Spohn, Herbert E.) *Encounter With Reality.* Boston: Houghton-Mifflin, 1968.

5. *Human Potentialities.* New York: Basic Books, Inc., 1958.

6. *Personality: A Biosocial Approach to Origins and Structure.* New York: Harper and Brothers, 1947.

7. "Self-Realization and Mental Health." *Bulletin of the Menninger Clinic.* 2 No. 3 (May 1959).

Rogers, Carl R.

8. "The Actualizing Tendency in Relation to 'Motives' and to Consciousness" in *Nebraska Symposium on Motivation,* Vol. 4. Marshall R. Jones, ed. Lincoln: University of Nebraska Press, 1963.

9. *Client-Centered Therapy.* Boston: Houghton-Mifflin Co., 1951.

10. *On Becoming a Person.* Boston: Houghton-Mifflin, 1961.

11. A Theory of Therapy, Personality, and Interpersonal Relationships as Developed in the Client-Centered Framework. In *Psychology: A Study of Science,* Vol. III, *Foundations of the Person in the Social Context,* Koch, ed. New York: McGraw-Hill, 1959.

12. "Toward A Science of the Person." *In Behaviorism and Phenomenology, Contrasting Basis for Modern Psychology,* T. W. Wann, ed. Chicago: University of Chicago Press, 1964.

6

Three Theories of
Healthy Personality

ABRAHAM MASLOW'S THEORY OF
HEALTHY PERSONALITY

Abraham Maslow's concepts of healthy personality are deeply embedded in the matrix of his theory of man's intrinsic nature and potentials for growth. In this respect, with the exception of the
strength of emphasis upon genetic components, he is not atypical of
other holistic theorists.

Man, as Maslow (3,9) views him, pursues life within the context
of an instinctoid need hierarchy which covers the full range and
spectrum of human desire and potential; from the hunger driven
man seeking food to human joy in the experience of aesthetic ecstasy. The prepotent needs, respectively, for physiological satisfaction, safety, love, self-esteem, and self-actualization emerge in a
relatively ordered and predictable sequence as each, in turn, is
gratified. Thus, the unfolding of the human potential is viewed from
a concept of progressive *need gratification* that provides theoretical
support for careful attention to the facilitation, accommodation
and satiation of fundamental needs while offering theoretical dis-
approval for their frustration or punishment. Instinctoid need frustration, in a real and lawful sense, produces psychopathology. The
reasoned acceptance of the need gratification theory rests upon
Maslow's conviction that the inner core of personality, in its nas-
cent state, is good, trustworthy, and ethical and must be allowed to
assert itself. Negative or destructive behaviors are epiphenomena,
symptoms resulting from a denial or deprivation of these needs. In
summary, if the gratification of the "lower" more basic instinctoid
needs proceeds without serious interruption, they become secondary and lose much of their compelling and controlling force in the
life of the organism. Attention, therefore, gradually moves beyond
these deficiency motivations to a heightened awareness of "higher,"
though biologically weaker, urges as new demands and expanded

possibilities emerge from ground into figure. As these "higher" instinctoid needs emerge they give rise to basic changes in the motivational structure of the organism in the conative-affective and cognitive areas in respect to character traits and in the dimension of interpersonal behavior (3).

BECOMING AND BEING: TWO BASIC HEALTH MODES

Although touched upon in Chapter 5, we need to distinguish more precisely between Maslow's two basic health modes, *becoming* and *being*, and clarify their relationship. Both modes incorporate essential aspects of healthy personality. *Becoming* is a directional, growth-centered process, a process that may span and encompass the full hierarchical range of instinctoid needs, both "lower" and "higher." In the healthy personality, it is a lifelong process of need transcendence; of increasing growth, change, and maturity. While both *becoming* and *being* are essential dimensions of healthy personality, *becoming* is conceptually subordinant since it facilitates, almost as a prerequisite, higher levels of self-actualization leading to forms of pure "being" (9). *Becoming* may contain some of the attributes of instrumental striving and coping behavior. For example, the individual's highly motivated efforts to achieve autonomy often become a means-centered struggle with the environment. In the early stages of growth, too, there is frequently the ubiquitous frustration of deficiency needs that must be resolved. *Becoming*, therefore, represents a life-long project that may transcend the deficiency motivations and enter into a more self-actualizing status while states of pure *being* are relatively temporary and unmotivated end-experiences. These latter experiences are rooted in immediacy and are largely expressive and "useless." Such "episodes" of *being* often represent a passive, receptive state that allows the organism a fully integrated expression of his potentials and an expression of his most unique and stylistic features, as in art, music, nature, interpersonal communication, and sex.

The pinnacle of human integration, experiencing, and personality achievement is reached in the full emergence and expression of these metamotivations. Theoretically, in the hierarchical arrangement of instinctoid needs, this apex of personal development presupposes that the "lower" more basic and prepotent needs have been adequately gratified, taken for granted, and receded into the "ground" of motivational dynamics. Thus, the higher needs emerg as "figure" and represent an advanced stage of self-actualization, a fuller, more complete realization of the human potential. Healthy personality, therefore, gradually emerges as a consequence of the organism's increased freedom for unmotivated experiencing and behavior. [1] The highest motives are, paradoxically, unmotivated.

In an interpretation of Maslow's theory of healthy personality, it is important to stress once more that these two basic modes of health, *becoming* and *being* are not mutually exclusive or antagonistic at the higher levels of human development. In the early stages of growth, moreover, a breakdown in the forward movement of the *becoming* process will certainly preclude a later realization of the higher instinctoid potentials for *being*. In most respects *becoming* and *being* are highly interdependent and mutually facilitating; healthy growth and becoming enhances or releases certain highly integrated moments or states of *being* which, in turn, stimulate further progress and the course of *becoming*.

"It looks as if human beings must be able both to affirm themselves (to be stubborn, stiff-necked, vigilant, alert, dominant, aggressive, self-confident, etc.) and also to be able to trust, to relax and to be receptive and Taoistic, to let things happen without interfering, to be humble and surrender." [2]

Autonomous Development

According to Maslow, the human being is in the possession of intrinsic laws that are distinguishable from those of natural reality, a non-human reality. While concessions must be made to the environment, these intrinsic laws of the organism deserve unconditional respect so that man is defined and understood intrapsychically rather than subjected to some extrapsychic, environment-centered criteria of mental health. Healthy personality, while including success in appropriate coping behavior, mastery, effectance, and com-

---

[1] In a recent observation representing an important shift in his theoretical position, Maslow (7) rejects an earlier assumption, inherent in his hierarchical theory of needs, that metamotivation comes about automatically as deficiency needs are resolved. Maslow now feels that there are other requirements and that basic need gratification is a necessary but not a sufficient condition to release the individual for self-actualization. One major factor in determining the level of development reached lies, perhaps, in the strength of the individual's 'impulse voices." The self-actualizing person exhibits a strong, "life positive" orientation that reflects the strength of the growth need throughout the entire need hierarchy. For a more complete discussion of this issue, see interview with Abraham Maslow.

[2] Abraham Maslow, "Lessons from the Peak-Experience," *Journal of Humanistic Psychology* 2 (1962): p. 16.

petence must also include a trancendence of the environment, an
independence of it, and a resistance to enculturation. A person who
gives in too readily to the distorting forces in the culture
may be less healthy than one who actively resists such forces. The
instinctoid needs are not created by the environment and Maslow
adamantly rejects the doctrine that one's conscience, rationality,
and ethics are little more than an acquired veneer. These characteristics of man are an integral part of his instinctoid nature, however submerged, disguised, or distorted they may appear to be.
Maslow emphasizes the autonomous nature of this inner character
and ethical potential of man and he provides evidence to indicate
that ". . . the organism is more trustworthy, more self-protecting,
self-directing, and self-governing than it is usually given credit
for." [3] Self-actualization and the accompanying metamotivations
are genetically based, the culmination of an intrinsic growth process and successful movement through a hierarchy of latent potentials, values, and needs.

Maslow (3) recognizes the Aristotelian and Spinozist parallels to
this concept of human nature but he contends that some crucial
distinctions must be made if we are to make a point of the comparison. He stresses that much more is known today about human
nature than in Aristotle's time and there is significantly more insight into man's potentials as well as more respect for the limitations of man's rational powers in achieving self-realization and the
good life.

One of the important implications of Maslow's instinctoid need
theory is that it points, quite logically, to a species-wide theory of
psychological health, to the development of universal criteria, as
Fromm (1) also suggests, for mental health.

Health as the Transcending of Dichotomies

A total investment of human energy into the requirements of a
given area of deficiency and frustration, i.e., a craving for love, a
neurotic search for comfort and security, etc., leaves the individual
compartmentalized and dissociated from crucial aspects of himself
as a full and whole being. Living with such a deficiency status precludes personality process and integration. Gratification in these

---

[3] Abraham Maslow, *Motivation and Personality* (New York: Harper & Row, 1954), p. 124.

crucial need areas, however, releases the individual for more advanced stages of human development which are marked by a more total experiencing of the self and the environment. The organism is gradually freed from the dehumanizing influences of the anxious struggle for survival.

One of the hallmarks of achieving a more fully actualized level of development, free from the concrete, dictatorial demands of the deficiency needs, is an increasing resolution of stereotyped conflicts and the transcending of age-old dichotomies that have pathologized much of life but long accepted as a normal expression of human nature. All "opposites," suggests Maslow (9), are hierarchically integrated in healthy people.

One of the chief criteria for the self-actualizing person, therefore, and a major theme in the writings of Maslow, is the resolution and transcendence of conflicts and dichotomies. In achieving this Gestalt, traditional problems become non-problems in the healthy personality.

The competitive and conflictual elements inherent in such polarities as rationality-impulse, means-ends, cognitive-conative, selfish-unselfish, primary process-secondary process, self-society, active-passive, masculine-feminine, duty-pleasure, work-play, spiritual-sensual, science-religion and the mystic-realistic, are problems only for unhealthy people. These poorly integrated conditions, however, are easily regarded as "normal" since they remain very much a part of the psychopathology of the "average" person. In addition to the resolution of the above dichotomies many traditional role conflicts tend to disappear such as the issues of incompatibility between age and youth, teacher and student, parent and child. These and many other conflicts are transcended in the well integrated personality. Significant channels for communication and relationship are thereby opened that are closed to most other individuals. In self-actualizing personalities these traditionally regarded incompatibles and opposites are resolved and the polarities disappear, leading to new levels of unity and wholeness. A newly ordered synthesis emerges and a synergic union of many apparent dichotomies is achieved.

These synergic developments are not abstract "intellectual" achievements functioning in a compartmentalized fashion but, rather, become genuine and pervasive characteristics and expressions of the total personality; an integral part of the most basic dynamics and psychological processes of the organism. Qualitative changes, too, become apparent in cognition and perception. "Being" cognition replaces the deficiency-oriented cognitions (Maslow, 9,4). Perceptions become less and less controlled by habitual "staticized" abstractions and are replaced by a more unique and idiosyncratic cognitive system that can deal with a "flux-and-process" reality rather than forcing a dynamic-process world into fixed and static states with need determined, autistic perceptions (Maslow, 3,9). *Increasing health, therefore, is reflected in perceptions of higher unity.* Thus, the common practice of categorizing, prejudging, and stereotyping flows from an ego-centered deficiency status with the need to force attributes of security, familiarity, and sameness, a certain manageability, onto a unique and dynamic world-in-process. The healthy personality is problem-centered, open to both the unknown and the unknowable. His openness and his freshness of perception, like the naive, unspoiled perceptions of a child, are the foundations of creativity, a common attribute of the healthy personality. To the frustrated and deprived organism an openness to such cognitions and perceptions is too threatening. The deficiency motivated personality finds his solace and perhaps his strength in an artificially created, simplistic universe, in stereotypes, and in a static, polarized world.

One of the most pervasive conflicts throughout history, the individual vs. society, may represent the ultimate in conflict resolution and synergy if a rapprochement can be effected. This would require a pluralistic society geared to the basic need satisfactions of its members and with a commitment to a philosophy that would offer not only a fundamental respect for the emergence of all attributes of self-actualization but a utilization of these attributes for its larger goals and purposes thereby creating a partnership between the individual and society. In such a synergistic relationship the interests of the individual are compatible with the fundamental goals and interests of the society and vice versa (6). This relationship provides a good example of the resolution of the dichotomy between selfishness and unselfishness. Achieving such a synergistic relationship between the individual and society would serve as one important measure of the healthy society.

The Peak-Experience

The supreme experience of pure *being* is discovered in the receptive phenomenon of the peak-experience. These ultimate expressions of healthy personality are unmotivated moments when self-consciousness is lost and "all fears, inhibitions, all tensions, all weaknesses . . . left behind." [4] Accompanying this experience is some vision of the ultimate, a profound penetration of the truth and the essence of life, or a sense of complete gratification, a feeling of perfection, and a validation of one's nature.

The peak-experience is an intense episode of self-actualization and, for Maslow, the sine qua non of healthy personality. Maslow (9) conceives of the peak-experience as the ultimate experience in unity and wholeness of the personality and a model of its highest potential. It is also a supreme identity experience when we are the most authentic and most deeply fulfilling the concept "human being." The peak-experience represents the emergence of latent aspects of a deeper inner nature that is seldom recognized and often persists unnoticed and undeveloped.

In their broadest significance, Maslow recognizes the peak, ecstatic moments in life as "core-religious" experiences but emerging as expressions of man's own instinctoid nature, the culmination of certain growth forces and a reflection of his higher need levels and potentials. In this manner, the peak-experience is seen as a naturalistic phenomenon, with biological sanctions, rather than interpreted within a supernatural context. In its deepest meaning, however, Maslow (5) does place a religious connotation on the experience. The religious quests, the religious yearnings are deeply rooted in human nature and are, therefore, perfectly respectable scientifically.

Maslow hypothesizes that many individuals, including neurotics, have been participants in the phenomenon of the peak-experience though the experience is denied or goes unrecognized by many. Theoretically, however, the greater the degree of self-actualization along a continuum of *becoming* the greater the frequency and depth of the peak-experiences. Here, again, we encounter the interdependent link between *becoming* and *being*. The higher the

[4] Maslow, *"Lessons From the Peak Experiences,"* p. 9.

level of *becoming* reached in the organism's autonomous, need-gratifying and ego-strengthening pursuits, in its successful coping and
"coming-to-terms" with the environment, the freer and more open
he or she becomes to transcend or "lose" the self in an isomorphic
union with the world. Self-transcendence, therefore, presupposes
ego-strength (9). Maslow (5) also suggests that frequent peak-experiences, during which B-cognition takes place, can lead to the
heightened probability of B-cognition without peak-experiences.

The capacity to experience these profound moments of pure
being is the primary distinguishing feature between two kinds or
types of self-actualizing people identified by Maslow. In a recent
paper Maslow (8) contrasts the "merely healthy" self-actualizers
who have had no transcendent or peak-experiences with a more advanced group who find such experiences important and central in
their lives. [5] Maslow suggests that this latter group, moving beyond
the "merely healthy" level, will also reflect a different philosophy
of life and will exhibit a more creative orientation to its possibilities. While this recent observation by Maslow represents a minor inconsistency with our interpretation of becoming and being, it
gives added emphasis to our conclusion that the ultimate expressions of healthy personality are to be found in the depth and range
of new modes of experiencing that the organism can achieve; in the
expanded and integrated forms of relating and responding to self
and the world.

VALUES, HEALTH AND HUMAN NATURE

All values that are inherent concomitants in the emergence of
metamotivation, in the peak-experiences, in the most highly developed regions of self-actualization are intrinsic in the structure of
human nature. Man's intrinsic nature is laden with value. In Maslow's theory of a psychology of being, an emerging transpersonal
psychology, the values of self-actualizing people are considered as
expressions of higher, more pervasive, species-wide needs. In a
word, though culturally nurtured, they are instinctoid and embedded in the biogenetic material of human nature. The intrinsic
urge to self-actualize, to grow toward a more complete realization

---

[5] For a discussion of this issue refer to the interview with Abraham Maslow.

of psychological health and *being*, ". . . means pressing toward what most people would call good values, toward serenity, kindness, courage, honesty, love, unselfishness, and goodness." [6]

Maslow's *being* psychology is a study of ideal states, states of perfection, of unitive consciousness, and the God-like aspects of the human being. More specifically, *being psychology* interprets the B-values, i.e., the being values, as the metamotivations of the human being (2). Maslow (4) lists the B-values, characteristics of the ideal, as follows: (1) Truth (2) Goodness (3) Beauty (4) Wholeness (4a) Dichotomy transcendence (5) Aliveness, process (6) Uniqueness (7) Perfection (7a) Necessity (8) Completion (9) Justice (9a) Order (10) Simplicity (11) Richness (12) Effortlessness (13) Playfulness (14) Self-sufficiency (15) Meaningfulness. Thus, the tasks of self-actualization, the metamotivations, are embodiments of intrinsic human values, rather than means-centered culturally-derived expedients. According to Maslow (5,7), spiritual and moral values have naturalistic meaning. We no longer need to rely on supernatural concepts to validate them.

A comprehensive definition of human nature, of the human potential, must include the intrinsic, instinctoid values, the components of the spiritual life. An actualization of these values is needed to avoid illness and to achieve full humanness. In a real sense, psychopathology is a value illness.

> The spiritual life is then part of the human essence. It is a defining characteristic of human nature, without which human nature is not full human nature. It is part of the Real Self, of one's identity, of one's inner core, of one's specieshood, of full-humanness. [7]

The species-wide B-values, the metaneeds, are not merely epiphenomena accruing from the satisfaction of lower values. They exist, though with less potency, as biological and psychological realities. The failure, therefore, to live a life that promotes, encourages and gives expression to these higher levels of *being* results in the activation of our "intrinsic conscience" and leads to "intrinsic guilt." Both are biological danger signals of value starvation (7). They are

---

[6] Abraham Maslow, *Toward a Psychology of Being* (Princeton: D. Van Nostrand, 1962), p. 147.
[7] Abraham Maslow, "A Theory of Metamotivation: The Biological Rooting of the Value Life," *Journal of Humanistic Psychology* 7 (1967): p. 113.

the natural and inevitable responses to self-betrayal, and serve as an internal warning to honor and respect one's nature.

Maslow (9) urges three directions of research to explore more fully the relationship between healthy personality and the nature of the B-values. *First,* he suggests that a greater number of psychologically healthy individuals be carefully selected for study as well as urging a study of the peak-experiences of a large number of individuals who may be at various levels along the need hierarchy. The higher values, the eternal verities, will be the free choices of many of these individuals. *Second,* we need to look more carefully at the diminution of value and at the process of spiritual regression as a person moves away from health into illness. *Finally,* we must research the changing orientation of those individuals in psychotherapy specifically seeking to move from sickness toward health.

In summary, healthy personality is achieving an articulation and actualization of one's inherent, naturalistic value system which must include the higher values, the B-values, in accord with the inherent spiritual sensitivity of human nature. The major expression of such an actualization is found in the peak-experience.

GARDNER MURPHY'S THEORY OF
HEALTHY PERSONALITY

Healthy personality for Gardner Murphy must ultimately reflect man's curiosity, his ubiquitous urges toward self-world discovery and understanding. In the realization of Murphy's third human nature, [8] the experience of the urgency to discovery and passion to explore and understand, the raw undisciplined energies and tension systems of man's most primitive nature are creatively channelled and given meaning and direction. The inertia and rigidity of cultural forms, "the chrysalis," is shattered, reshaped, and revitalized.

Against the evolutionary background of the three human natures, Murphy (11) posits two basic or universal tendencies within the human organism which give intrinsic satisfactions without excessive conflict with other tendencies.

---

[8] Refer to the discussion of Murphy's treatment of the holistic theme of *Process,* Chapter 4.

1. *General affection:* out-going warmth, social feeling, generosity, and sympathy.

2. *Cognitive-affective tendencies:* an intense curiosity and interest in the world of discovery, a joy in creating, understanding and mastering. These cognitive-affective tendencies reflect an inherent reality-seeking orientation, a demand to apprehend the "real."

While recognizing the human need for safety, for an ordered expression of the basic human tendencies, and a protection against the unknown, Murphy considers a significant part of the essential nature of humanness to lie in the organism's evolutionary growth trends toward unresolved balances and the creation of disorder and instability. Healthy personality as well as a viable society must remain an "unfinished canvas." The great challenge today, Murphy feels, is to provide for the flow of drives and human expression without making "irrecoverable investments" in any one form or formula. Above all, the human mind must remain open, curious, and unsatiated. Vigilant effort is required to maintain such openness since it is a much more difficult achievement than developing order and stability and a comfortable point of view.

In judging the value of the vast array of human endeavors and pursuits, Murphy's criteria require that such involvements make one more sensitive to new experience and enrich capacities leading to deeper and deeper satisfactions in both the social sphere and the cognitive-affective world.

The various expressions of healthy personality, therefore, have a universal linkage with the nature and potentials of the human organism. The highest aspirations of man are, inexorably, "an expression of the kind of tissues of which he is made up." [9] Murphy suggests that the supposition of universal value directions deserves very serious consideration and study, the crucial question being ". . . what sorts of things does any species *tend to learn;* what are the lines of development which it follows when it does what it wants to do?" [10]

The healthy personality, sensitized to his craving for understanding and discovery, engages in new modes of experience and

---

[9] Gardner Murphy, *Personality: A Biosocial Approach to Origins and Structure* (New York: Harper and Brothers, 1947), p. 48.
[10] Gardner Murphy, *Human Potentialities* (New York: Basic Books, 1958), p. 308.

". . . which constitutes independent, unconventional, non-routinized, original thought." [11] The healthy personality is thus engaged in the process of challenging assumptions, thereby adding new dimensions [12] and new systems of realities to an evolving never-to-be finished individuality. The healthy personality is free from the assertion that "there is nothing new under the sun" and is forever open to the emergence and recognition of new or latent potentialities. A "mood," a "feeling quality" provides an affective direction, a certain readiness for discovery, for movement toward these goals. Interests flow outward to include more and more attributes of the world (11). To discover is fulfilling and it is this fulfillment via the sensory, motor, or intellectual modes which the emerging third human nature seeks. Healthy personality, therefore, can never be realized by a quantitative extension of current themes or trends.

COSMIC CONSCIOUSNESS

It is the openness to experience and commitment to an experimental orientation to life that frees man and puts him in touch with the universe and the ultimate realities such as an isomorphic union bestows.

Man is *"a part of the sweep of the cosmos"* [13] and it is this deep affinity with cosmic materials and structure that is the potential source of man's deepest and richest fulfillment. This organismic affinity can be seen early in the child's life as he responds spontaneously to cosmic patterns as an integral part of his self-structure. For Murphy (12,11), therefore, one of the highest developments and expressions of the human personality is to become one with the cosmos, to become sensitive to and resonate with cosmic structure. It is achieved through a discovery of those harmonic links between internal needs, tensions, cycles, and rhythms and the outer cosmic realities. This heightened identification with the cosmos requires the development of one's potentials, an intimate self-awareness and an ego equipped to deal with cosmic reality. There must be an exploration and discovery of the qualities of the self that resonate most deeply with world elements so that appropriate modes of inter-

---

[11] *Ibid.*, p. 128.

[12] Dimension is defined by Murphy as a new perspective, a "way of grasping," a new world of meaning and value.

[13] Murphy, *Human Potentialities*, p. 23.

action and integration can occur. "Personality is as much a *way of becoming sensitive* as it is a way of reacting upon the environment." [14]

According to Murphy, the achievement of cosmic consciousness may be expressed in states of selflessness and in a variety of loss-of-self phenomena exhibiting a freeing and extension of traditional ego boundaries. There is the apprehension of a higher reality as self becomes undifferentiated from world. A state of ecstasy is characteristic of most such experiences (10). Murphy interprets the process of achieving states of cosmic consciousness thus:

> . . . along with the greatly increased sensitivity to many aspects of the universe there is a loss of the sense of contrast or opposition between the self and the world. The content of self *is*, then, the world content; one is caught up in the joy of union with the cosmos.[15]

All contacts and interactions with the environment, indeed, all reality has a self-reference. The person's experience of cosmic consciousness, therefore, will be a unique and selective one and not a facsimile of all such experiences of others. ". . . rather, he would become more individuated, selecting from the cosmos what is deeply significant of himself." [16] Isomorphism thus allows for the uniqueness of individual structure and autonomy while providing a resonance of inner with outer structure. Murphy (11) suggests that such cosmic unions are often "unmotivated" states, "unproductive" moments of the relaxed, casual and exploratory.

States of cosmic consciousness represent an integration of the three human natures, the instinctual, the formal, and the sensory, giving rise to the most "profound arousal" [17] and the formation of a new emergent whole. Thus, the growth potentials and the power of the transforming character of such cosmic experiences is emphasized.

> It is because of man's capacity for intimate union with the stuff of this world through the methods of the arts and through the methods of science that he may hope to do more than to transcend himself, may hope to become in each new emergent phase of his life a new kind of man.[18]

---

[14] Murphy, *Personality*, p. 112.
[15] *Ibid.*, p. 521.
[16] Gardner Murphy and Herbert E. Spohn, *Encounter with Reality* (Boston: Houghton Mifflin Company, 1968), p. 122 ff.
[17] Murphy, *Human Potentialities*, p. 184.
[18] *Ibid.*, p. 325.

This supreme achievement of self-realization is not a hedonistic, self-indulgent development. Murphy considers it a positive phase of socialization since a craving for the social is a real and vital component of human nature. Man seeks to establish contact with reality. A failure in social communication and fulfillment, therefore, represents a major failure in the achievement of human nature itself. Murphy (11) rejects any concept of self-realization that disallows this inexorable link between man and his environment and the social nature of psychological reality. He suggests that an experience of ecstasy may be achieved in an interaction and sense of communion between two or more selves and he states that ". . . a healthy personality is largely . . . a system of interpersonal relations involving acceptance, affection, encouragement, and belief in one another." [19]

CARL ROGERS' THEORY OF HEALTHY PERSONALITY

Of fundamental importance in the life of the organism, any organism, is an active, progressive striving in the direction of maintaining, enhancing, and reproducing itself. This most salient feature in human motivation, the *actualizing tendency,* the "central source of energy," [20] is defined by Rogers as

> . . . the inherent tendency of the organism to develop all its capacities in ways which serve to maintain or enhance the organism. . . . Development toward the differentiation of organs and functions, expansion and enhancement through reproduction. It is development toward autonomy and away from heteronomy, or control by external forces.[21]

In addition, a basic component of the *actualizing tendency* is expressed by the organism's need to establish a unity or wholeness of personality and maintain a self-consistency by keeping the self--

---

[19] Gardner Murphy, "Self-Realization and Mental Health," *Bulletin of the Menninger Clinic* 23, No. 3 (1959): p. 83.

[20] *Carl R. Rogers.* "Actualizing Tendency in Relation to 'Motives' and Consciousness," in *Nebraska Symposium on Motivation,* ed. Marshall R. Jones (Lincoln: University of Nebraska Press, 1963), p. 6.

[21] Carl R. Rogers, "A Theory of Therapy, Personality and Interpersonal Relationships as Developed in the Client-Centered Framework," in *Psychology: A Study of A Science,* Vol. 3, ed. S. Koch (New York: McGraw-Hill, 1959), p. 196.

concept congruent or compatible with experience and by the capacity to experience in awareness the discrepancies that develop between the self-concept and experience. It is a veritable requirement for the healthy organism to symbolize experience accurately in awareness (15). Beyond this sovereign directional tendency Rogers feels no need to postulate any additional or "higher" motive in his theoretical system. An unswerving commitment to this autonomous, selective direction of the organism supports Rogers' faith in the individual's capacity for self-guidance, self-direction, and competence. He views the natural expressions of the *actualizing tendency* as a reliable and constructive force in the life of the organism. The most organic, most basic strivings and needs of man are positive and constructive in nature.

In working out an expression of Rogers' theory of healthy personality, a second motivational tendency must be introduced. This additional motivational construct, *the tendency toward self-actualization*, is an auxiliary expression of the *actualizing tendency* of the organism and manifests itself, following early developments of the self-structure, by actualizing or enhancing those aspects of experience which are symbolized as a part of the self (Rogers, 15, 13). As we shall see, these may be the learned constructs in experience leading to incongruence or they may represent more genuine values and directions emerging from the full-range of experiences of the organism guided by the actualizing tendency. It is the relationship between these two basic tendencies that leads to the health process of the fully-functioning person or to the arrested development of the poorly integrated personality.

THE DEVELOPMENT OF CONGRUENCE

The development of a relative state of *congruence* is essential to the development of healthy personality. Indeed, Rogers treats healthy personality and congruence as synonymous states. Rogers defines *congruence* as a condition of the personality "when self-experiences are accurately symbolized, and are included in the self-concept in this accurately symbolized form." [22]

The personality ingredients for the development of congruence,

---

[22] *Ibid.*, p. 206.

in addition to the *actualizing tendency* and the *tendency toward self-actualization* include an early acquired secondary need for *positive regard*. This need may be met in a manner leading to a congruent or incongruent state of the personality. In the normal development of *congruence* the child is "prized" and experiences the genuine expression and communication of *unconditional positive regard* from significant others in his life. There are no conditions attached to his acceptance and worth as a person. The child is not confronted with bargains to make, or with demands for personal sacrifice in exchange for love. If these conditions are maintained the individual becomes free to evolve and develop from the deeply-rooted base of the actualizing tendency and his own organismic experiencing so that there is, ideally, always an accurate matching of experience and awareness and virtually no need for the development of a defensive organization. In this condition of congruence it is clear that the developing self-structure is highly compatible with the experiences of the organism. Thus, both the *actualizing tendency* and *tendency toward self-actualization* are in harmony and mutually supporting an evolving self-structure that is rooted more and more deeply in the organismic experiencing of the person.

In congruence, then, there is a high compatibility between the self as perceived and actual experience. Experiences are accurately and clearly symbolized in awareness, recognized and acknowledged as facets of the self, and appropriately incorporated into the self-structure. Thus, the *tendency toward self-actualization* is in the service of the *actualizing tendency*.

Rogers emphasizes the process character, the directional nature of the congruent personality and he characterizes the self structure of the fully functioning person as a "fluid gestalt" [23] always in the process of change and engaged in the assimilation of new experience. Thus, congruence is not a static state as Rogers sees it but requires periodic revision of the self-concept to bring it in line with accurately symbolized experience. "Optimal psychological adjustment is thus synonymous with complete congruence of self and experience." [24]

---

[23] Rogers, A *Theory of Therapy, Personality, and Interpersonal Relationships*, in *Psychology*, ed. S. Koch, p. 234.

[24] *Ibid.*, p. 206.

Few lives, if any, approximate Rogers' ideal of congruence. More often, a condition of *incongruence* prevails so that there is some discrepancy between the organism's authentic experience and what he feels free to symbolize in awareness as a part of the self. This state of incongruence comes about when conditions of worth are imposed upon the individual. Under this influence of *conditional* positive regard from significant others, the individual is encouraged to deny important aspects of his own experience in order to meet his need for positive regard and the requirements for conditional love. He thus becomes alienated from the springs of his own being and two conflicting motivational systems become operative. The *tendency toward self-actualization* persists but becomes dissociated, estranged from the inherent *actualizing tendency*. The actualizing tendency is subverted and its energies lend support to learned behaviors, feelings, and values that do not actualize the individual. Rejecting the validity of his own experiencing he often becomes his own worst enemy, at war with himself. There is a deep conflict between the intellectual structure of experience and the unrecognized valuing process going on within. He gradually loses contact with the wisdom of his own processes and basic tendencies (13). As the individual adopts, symbolizes in awareness, and actualizes more and more of those conditions of worth that are required of him or communicated to him he becomes increasingly estranged from the voices of his own experience. The developing self-structure and organismic experience have become incongruent. Rogers (13) sees this condition as the beginning of personality disintegration and the basis of all psychological pathology.

Concomitant with a high degree of congruence is an organismic valuing process guided by the *actualizing tendency*. Rogers compares adult maturity and the achievement of congruence with the natural strivings and expressions of the human infant where every impulse, selection, and choice is in the positive direction of maintaining and enhancing the organism. Thus, in both the congruent, fully-functioning adult and the naturally congruent state of the infant there is a basic trust in one's experiencing.

This organismic valuing process in the mature person is not always a stable and fixed system but one that discriminates and establishes priority on the basis of the values facilitating the growth and actualization of the organism (16). In an internal state of congruence, the source of such a valuing process is clearly within the individual and in harmony with his own experience. Unlike the neurotic or dissociated personality, it is not a rigid, abstract, and intellectually structured value system external to experience and based primarily upon arbitrary demands and expectations, upon "conceived values" introjected from the conditional positive regards of others.[25] Thus, according to Rogers, values of the healthy personality are changing and highly differentiated, their reorganizations following the time, flow, and meaning of experience. In the congruent or healthy personality, therefore, the rational selections and intellectual value choices are in essential harmony with the organism's intuitive and affective valuing process.

It is apparent that the issue of the universality of values is a substantive one in Rogers' theory and he suggests that ". . . we have the possibility of universal human value directions *emerging* from the experiencing of the human organism." [26] In individuals moving toward congruence, toward greater openness to their experience, there is an "organismic commonality" of value directions that (a) fosters the process of self-actualization, (b) enhances the development of others in the community, (c) strives to maintain the survival and the evolution of the species (16). It is clear, although Rogers has been misunderstood or misinterpreted on this point, that the actualizing tendency is not a hedonistic and self-centered process of development frequently acting at the expense of others (14, 17).

The healthy personality, Rogers' "fully-functioning" person, is the theoretical end-point of therapy. The observed value directions of clients in psychotherapy, therefore, have served as one major source of evidence for universal human value directions and are considered to be important process or directional characteristics of the healthy growth of the personality. Rogers perceives his clients to be moving in the following directions:

---

[25] Rogers employs "value" in the usage of C. Morris' "operative values," in which the behavior of organisms show preference for one object or objective rather then another, in contrast to "conceived values," where there is preference for a symbolized object, (i.e., honesty is the best policy), and "objective value," that which is objectively preferable whether or not it is sensed or conceived of as personally desirable.

[26] Carl Rogers, "Toward A Modern Approach to Values: The Valuing Process in the Mature Person," *Journal of Abnormal and Social Psychology* 68 (1964): p. 167.

(1) away from facades, (2) away from "oughts," (3) away from meeting the expectations of others, (4) toward valuing "being real," (5) toward valuing self-direction, (6) toward valuing one's self and feelings, (7) toward valuing being as process, (8) toward a greater valuing of others, (9) toward a valuing of deeper, more intimate relationships, (10) toward a greater valuing of an openness to all inner and outer experiences (16, 14).

> I believe that when the human being is inwardly free to choose whatever he deeply values, he tends to value those objects, experiences, and goals which make for his own survival, growth and development, and for the survival and development of others.[27]

---

[27] Rogers, *Toward a Modern Approach to Values*, p. 166.

References

Fromm, Eric.

1. *The Sane Society.* New York: Holt, Rinehart, and Winston, 1955.

Maslow, Abraham.

2. "Further Notes on the Psychology of Being," *Journal of Humanistic Psychology* 3 (1963): 120–135.
3. *Motivation and Personality.* New York: Harper and Row, 1954.
4. "Notes on Being Psychology," *Journal of Humanistic Psychology* 2 (1962): 47–71.
5. *Religions, Values, and Peak Experiences.* Columbus: Ohio State University Press, 1964.
6. "Synergy in the Society and in the Individual," *Journal of Individual Psychology* 20 (1964): 153–164.
7. "A Theory of Metamotivation: The Biological Rooting of the Value-Life," *Journal of Humanistic Psychology* 7, No. 2 (1967): 93-127.
8. Theory Z. In *New Developments Within the Human Side of Enterprise,* W. G. Bennie and E. H. Schein, eds. New York: McGraw-Hill, 1969.
9. *Toward a Psychology of Being.* Princeton: D. Van Nostrand Co., Inc., 1962.

Murphy, Gardner.

10. *Encounter with Reality.* (with Spohn, Herbert E.) Boston: Houghton-Mifflin, 1968.
11. *Human Potentialities.* New York: Basic Books, Inc., 1958.
12. *Personality: A Biosocial Approach to Origins and Structure.* New York: Harper and Brothers, 1947.

Rogers, Carl.

13. "The Actualizing Tendency in Relation to 'Motives' and to Consciousness." *Nebraska Symposium on Motivation,* vol. 4, Marshall R. Jones, ed. Lincoln: University of Nebraska Press, 1963.
14. *On Becoming a Person.* Boston: Houghton-Mifflin, 1961.
15. "A Theory of Therapy, Personality, and Interpersonal Relationships as Developed in the Client-Centered Framework." *Psychology: A Study of A*

Science, vol. 3, *Foundations of the Person in the Social Context.* S. Koch, ed. New York: McGraw-Hill, 1959.

16. "Toward A Modern Approach to Values: The Valuing Process in the Mature Person." *Journal of Abnormal and Social Psychology* 68, No. 4 (1964): 160–167.

Storr, A.

17. *The Integrity of the Personality.* Baltimore: Penguin Books, 1963.

BIOGRAPHICAL SKETCHES

ABRAHAM MASLOW

Dr. Abraham Maslow, internationally known educator and psychologist, was born in Brooklyn on April 1, 1908. He received his B.A., M.A., and Ph. D. (1934) degrees from the University of Wisconsin.

Out of his vigorous research and prolific writing has come much of the inspiration and impetus for the contemporary "third force" humanistic psychology movement with its emphasis upon freeing psychology from its rigidities in order to create a more human science. The name Abraham Maslow has become synonomous with these new concerns for a broader, more humanistically oriented psychology. These concerns, given little attention by existing theories and systems, are devoted to topics such as creativity, healthy personality, love and play, spontaneity, personal growth, and higher levels of consciousness. Dr. Maslow explored and expanded all of these areas in his writings.

Throughout his distinguished career, Dr. Maslow taught and lectured at major colleges and universities throughout the United States, Canada, and Mexico. In 1967–68 his outstanding accomplishments and contributions to the field of psychology were honored through his election to the Presidency of the American Psychological Association.

In addition to his classic work in motivation theory, *Motivation and Personality,* Dr. Maslow's major publications include *Toward a*

Psychology of Being; Religions, Values, and Peak Experiences; The Psychology of Science; and an edited volume, *New Knowledge in Human Values.* He was on the editorial boards of many leading journals and his articles appeared in a great variety of publications too numerous to mention.

Dr. Maslow's longest academic tenure was at Brandeis University. He went to Brandeis University in 1951 where he served as Chairman of the Psychology Department for ten years. In 1969, at the peak of his career and influence, Dr. Maslow took a leave of absence from Brandeis University to accept a four year research grant from the W. P. Laughlin Foundation in Menlo Park, California. During the period of this grant Dr. Maslow intended to develop "the philosophy of democratic politics, economics, and ethics which is generated by the humanistic psychology. . . ." After a year of work under this grant, Dr. Maslow died of a heart attack on June 8, 1970.

GARDNER MURPHY

Dr. Gardner Murphy was born in Chillicothe, Ohio in 1895. He received his B.A. degree from Yale University in 1916 with a major in Psychology. A year later he received his A. M. degree from Harvard University where he emphasized studies in personality, philosophy, and began a life-long study and interest in psychical research. Following a two year interruption for service with a Mobile Hospital Unit in France, Dr. Murphy continued his graduate study at Columbia University, developing a close association with Professor R.W. Woodworth. He received his Ph. D. in 1923.

In 1940, after a long tenure as student and professor at Columbia University, Dr. Murphy became professor and chairman of the Psychology Department at the City College of New York. In 1943–44 he served as President of the American Psychological Association.

Dr. Murphy has consistently exhibited a concern for social problems. In 1950 he served as a consultant to the government of India and to various Indian Universities dealing with a UNESCO study of "social tensions" in India.

In 1952 Dr. Murphy became Director of Research at The Menninger Foundation, Topeka, Kansas. In this capacity Dr. Murphy

directed important long-term research studies in perceptual learning, personality problems, and psychical research. In much of this
research the primary emphasis was upon determining the influence
of wishes, needs, and emotions on the way we perceive, remember,
and think. Dr. Murphy's formal association with the Menninger
Clinic lasted until 1965 when he retired as Director of Research.
Later, however, he was appointed as Henry March Pfeiffer professor and served as chief research consultant for two more years.

In 1967 Dr. Murphy became Visiting Professor of Psychology at
George Washington University. In the capacity of this present position, Dr. Murphy is concerned with bringing together the various
lines of thought relative to "self-deception." His recent publication
with Herbert E. Spohn, *Encounter With Reality*, represents a discussion of some of the basic issues in this area. He is also engaged in
studies in the psychology of international relations.

Dr. Murphy's major publications date back to 1929 when he
published *Historical Introduction to Modern Psychology*. In 1931,
with Lois B. Murphy, he published *Experimental Social Psychology*
with a revised edition appearing in 1937 (with Lois B. Murphy and
T. M. Newcomb.) Dr. Murphy's major publication, a scholarly and
now classic work in personality theory, is *Personality: A Biosocial
Approach to Origins and Structure* published in 1947. This work of-
fers a brilliant synthesis of all relevant personality theory and research that had accumulated by that time and it represents an integration of the important biological and social determinants of
personality. In 1962 Dr. Murphy gave expression to his life-long interest and commitment to psychic phenomena with the publication
of *Challenge of Psychical Research*. In much of this writing and research Dr. Murphy has worked in close collaboration with his wife,
Lois Barclay Murphy and in the areas of child psychology and personality they have worked together on the same problems.

Dr. Murphy's research and scholarship and the depth and
breadth of his knowledge in psychology and related fields is equaled
by few American psychologists. In addition, Dr. Murphy has
worked assiduously for a more open psychology and for a science of
man that is less constricted and freer to explore and experiment
with a greater variety of human problems and social phenomena.
Outside the "establishment" of psychology Dr. Murphy has pursued

his interest in psychical research to the dismay of the majority of his colleagues. His courageous efforts within his profession have been chiefly responsible for the credence now given to such phenomena and its growing acceptance among psychologists.

CARL ROGERS

Dr. Carl Rogers was born on January 8, 1902. He was a Phi Beta Kappa graduate of the University of Wisconsin, 1924. He entered Union Theological Seminary in 1924 where he spent two important formative years. Later, he began taking courses at Teachers College, Columbia University where he completed his Ph. D. degree in 1931 after several years of experience as a clinical psychologist and child guidance worker in Rochester, New York. In 1939-1940, during his last year in Rochester, Dr. Rogers served as Director of the Rochester Guidance Center. It was out of the early experience and experimentation in Rochester that came Rogers' first major publication, *Clinical Treatment of the Problem Child*, 1939.

Following the important years in Rochester which served as a base for later explorations, Dr. Rogers held increasingly important positions in psychology and positions of leadership in counseling centers. In 1940 Dr. Rogers went to Ohio State University as Professor of Psychology. During his tenure at Ohio State he published his first major presentation on client-centered counseling, *Counseling and Psychotherapy*, 1942.

In 1945 Dr. Rogers became Professor of Psychology and Executive Secretary of the Counseling Center, University of Chicago. He remained at the University of Chicago until 1957 when he took a professorial position at the University of Wisconsin in the Departments of Psychology and Psychiatry. During the Chicago years, Dr. Rogers stimulated and directed many important research projects on his emerging theories of personality and new approaches in psychotherapy. Dr. Rogers' next major publication, *Client-Centered Therapy*, 1951, developed, in large part, out of these experiences and research studies at the University of Chicago. In addition to these publications Dr. Rogers has published *On Becoming a Person*, 1961; *The Therapeutic Relationship and Its Impact: A Study of Psychotherapy with Schizophrenics* (with E. T. Gendlin, D. J. Kiesler, and C. B. Truax), 1967; and *Man and the Science of Man* (Ed., with Wm. R. Coulson), 1968. Dr. Rogers has also written other books and articles too numerous to mention. Many of his works have been translated into foreign languages, especially Japanese and French.

In 1963 Dr. Rogers became a Resident Fellow at Western Behavioral Sciences Institute in La Jolla, California. At the present time he is Resident Fellow of the Center for Studies of the Person, La Jolla, California.

Dr. Rogers is one of the most important and esteemed psychologists of our time. He has served as president of the American Psychological Association and is the only American psychologist to be awarded both of the major awards of that Association. In 1956, Dr. Rogers was awarded the Distinguished Scientific Contribution Award for his outstanding research in the field of psychotherapy. In 1968, Dr. Rogers received the Award for Professional Achievement, also from the American Psychological Association.

In recent years, in conjunction with his involvement at the Center for Studies of the Person, Dr. Rogers has been very active in the issues of education and in the encounter group movement. In the latter area, Dr. Rogers leads many encounter groups each year. Reflecting his interest in the problems of education and in the personal growth possibilities of small group interaction Dr. Rogers has recently published two books: *Freedom to Learn: A View of What Education Might Become*, 1969 and *Carl Rogers on Encounter Groups*, 1970.

In spite of his continued vigorous professional activity, this does not mark the limit of Carl Rogers' interest. As a dedicated photographer, he has taken pictures in many parts of the world. Currently, his major hobby is gardening with a special fondness for the tuberous begonia.